The Priesthood of All Believers

1st Century Church Life in the 21st Century

by
Milt Rodriguez

THE PRIESTHOOD OF ALL BELIEVERS

Published by

The Rebuilders

admin@therebuilders.org/www.therebuilders.org

Printed in the United States of America

Acknowledgement

There were three people who made the production of this book possible. I would like to thank them from the bottom of my heart.

The proofreading was done by Donna Sievers, Pamela Holland and Mary Rodriguez. Pamela spent long hours correcting all of my grammatical mistakes. Mary, my wife, spent many hours typing the manuscript and formatting the book. Thank you all so much.

TABLE OF CONTENTS

THE PRIESTHOOD OF ALL BELIEVERS

PREFACE

This book is written for you, the believer in Jesus Christ. It is the result of over twenty-five years of seeking God for insight concerning His eternal purpose and the role that the church has to play in that purpose. I am, by no means, an expert on these things; however, I feel that I do have a contribution to make.

The subject I attempt to approach in this book is most difficult because of the gross misunderstanding prevalent among believers today. Just writing the word "church" seems to conjure up many different images, feelings, and thoughts for different believers. When you just read that word, what thoughts came to your mind? For each of us, it will be a little (or a lot) different according to our backgrounds, religious training, education, and experience. The key to the breakthrough that is needed is the following question: "What does *God* mean when He says that word?"

There is no doubt that our thoughts are not His thoughts and His ways are much higher than our ways. Our thoughts and conceptions are riddled with corruption because of our fallen nature. The strongholds in our minds are built with the wood, hay, and stubble of man-made ideas. These strongholds can only be broken down as we are confronted with truth and then choose to take our thoughts captive to the obedience of Christ. Seeing God's perspective on this subject is the key to everything. After all, this whole thing is God's deal anyway. What I mean is, this is *His* eternal purpose and *His* church.

I firmly believe that we cannot understand His church before we understand His purpose. The church is here to fulfill God's eternal purpose and if we don't know what that purpose is, then how will we know how to fulfill it? You cannot understand how something functions unless you understand its purpose. If you thought that the purpose of an automobile was to fly in the air, then your whole mindset would be geared toward making that car fly. But that car was never designed to fly. It has another purpose. However, if you didn't know that purpose, then you would do everything in your power to make that thing fly. Perhaps you would attach some wings, or a propeller, or some such nonsense. You would end up trying to change that vehicle to suit your purpose and would end up with some strange contraption. That, my friends, is what we have done with the church.

I will tell you right now, that you will not get very far in this book if you will not open your mind and allow the Holy Spirit to give you God's thoughts and God's perspective on these matters. I will do my best to present to you the spiritual facts of the scriptures, but it will be up to you to open your mind and your spirit to allow those facts to take hold.

The spiritual "facts" that I am referring to is the pattern for the church that can be seen in the scriptures. God *does* have a pattern for the church. He *does* care how the church is built. This "pattern" is based upon life, divine life, not rigid organizational machinery. The principles of His life are the keys. It's a very simple pattern, as we will see, but it is a pattern nonetheless. All life has a pattern. Just take a look at biological life and you will see that it has a pattern. We call that pattern DNA. Your whole body is built upon the pattern or code contained within your DNA. Understand that code, and you go a long way to understanding the life of your body.

What we see in the scriptures is the record of the expression of divine life. The people who were involved with the living of this life wrote down what they observed. For example, Luke wrote for us a beautiful record of what he saw happening in the early church in the Book of Acts. He observed the expression of the life, and then wrote it down. The scriptures are the records of the divine life in action.

The problem is that we have taken these records and made them a rule book on how to have church. The records are there to instruct us and show us how divine life behaves, so that we will know the pattern by the expression. The life must come first!

You cannot get the life by imitating the expression. For example, we are told in Acts that the Jerusalem church sold all their possessions and laid them at the feet of the apostles. That was the way the life of Christ expressed itself in a particular instance. The idea is not to copy what they did in hopes of attaining their spiritual life. The point here is that this story shows us how divine life behaves. It reveals to us, in part, a little more of the pattern. Divine life always gives away its own life. This is not something that was instituted by Jesus in the "Sermon on the Mount," or by the church in Jerusalem. This is simply how God behaves! This originated inside of the Godhead. The Father is always giving away His life to His Son.

So what we see happening in Jerusalem is a "fleshing out" of His life. The life flowed out of the people and it took the form of certain actions. Let's not make the mistake of duplicating those actions in hopes of having the life. That's backwards. We need to learn how to live by His life and then the actions or expression will take care of itself. Life must always precede form. The form, structure, pattern, or whatever you want to call it, will always be determined by the life. Life always makes a way. If divine life is flowing, then an expression will result. That expression will be Christ, the corporate Christ. How could it not be? Your life expresses you, does it not? How could the life of Christ, freely flowing, not express the living Lord?

This is a point that I cannot stress enough. I will be making it over and over again throughout this book. Please do not read this book as a manual on how to do church. These "observations" are simply things I have seen of the pattern of divine life as revealed in the scriptures and in my own experiences.

Why does the church we see today look so different from the church we see in the New Testament? Have you ever found yourself asking that question? That's the question that started me on my journey. I had to take a completely new look at the scriptures and not read them through the filtered glasses of my own background and experiences. Even though I believe I have found the answers to many of the questions, I am still on that journey, the journey into the center of God's heart for His church.

So, if you will, join me on that journey as we take a look at God's eternal purpose, and the vehicle for that purpose; the Church of Jesus Christ.

The
Priesthood
of All
Believers

CHAPTER ONE

GOD'S ETERNAL PURPOSE

We live in a day when most believers don't really have a purpose. We have agendas, programs, causes, activities, and ministries, but we don't have a purpose. Of course, if you ask most believers if they have a purpose they will say yes. When you ask them what it is, they will proceed to tell you what their church is currently doing. Or they may give you some vague answer such as to do the will of God, or to glorify God. But the will of God is the same as saying the purpose of God, so in effect; they are telling you that their purpose is to fulfill His purpose! But what *is* His purpose?

Many others will tell you that God's will or purpose is to evangelize the world. That's why Jesus came, to save sinners, after all. Or perhaps it's healing, or deliverance, or to bring restoration to the family, or to this nation, or to the church. Yet none of these things even come close to describing God's eternal purpose. How do I know this? Simple, all of the above answers have to do with time and space. They all take place in creation, after the fall. Yet Paul tells us that God's purpose is *eternal*.

An Eternal Purpose

> "This was in accordance with the *eternal* purpose which He carried out (formed) in Christ Jesus our Lord . . ." Eph. 3:11

Eternal purpose here literally means "purpose of the ages." You see, this purpose, this will, this intention, this plan, has *always* been and *always* will be His purpose throughout *all* ages! Therefore, His purpose existed *before* there was man, or the fall, or creation. Therefore, His purpose cannot be to save the lost because this purpose is before (and after!) the fall of man. Of course, God *does* want to save the lost, and heal, and deliver, and all the other things that Christians love to focus on. But those things are not His eternal purpose. He had something in His mind and heart, before any of those things were necessary. He created the entire universe and all realms, visible and invisible, with this purpose in mind. This purpose is what motivates your God to do everything He does. It is the driving force behind creation, and salvation, and reconciliation. It is the reason why the church exists.

Please take note that God's purpose is singular. He has *a* purpose, not *many* purposes. Your God is single minded in this matter of His will and purpose. Please understand that in God's mind, all roads lead to this one single purpose. Everything He plans, and everything He does leads to the fulfillment of this single purpose. "Who worketh *all things* after the counsel of His own will." Eph. 1:11b

The Godhead took counsel together in eternity and decided

upon a great goal. All of the workings of God would revolve around this great goal. All of His hopes and expectations would move to this one great end. He would not stop until the fullness of His great purpose was realized. God is relentless and unswerving in His pursuit of this glorious quest.

The Importance of Revelation

You and I need a Spirit-borne revelation of His eternal purpose. Why? The answer is simple. How will we understand our purpose if we don't know (by revelation) His purpose? We are not here to fulfill our own purposes. We are here to fulfill *His* purpose.

> "And we know that God causes all things to work together for good to those who love God, to those who are called according to *His* purpose." Rom. 8:28

However, we need to *see* this purpose with our spiritual eyes. We need the Holy Spirit to give us a revelation of this wonderful purpose in our spirits. If we can truly "see" this purpose, it will be branded into our souls and we will never forget it. It will become the all-consuming passion of our lives. It will become the driving force behind everything we do, just like it is for our Father in heaven.

The Eternal Purpose Revealed

> "In Him we have redemption through His blood, the forgiveness of our trespasses,

according to the riches of His grace, which He lavished upon us. In all wisdom and insight He made known to us the mystery of His will, according to His kind intention which He purposed in Him with a view to an administration suitable to the fullness of the times, *that is, the summing up of all things in Christ*, things in the heavens and things upon the earth. In Him also we have obtained an inheritance, having been predestined according to His purpose who works all things after the counsel of His will, to the end that we who were the first to hope in Christ should be to the praise of His glory." Eph. 1:7-12

"And He put all things under His feet, and gave Him to be *head over all things* to the church, which is His body, the fullness *of Him who fills all in all*." Eph. 1:22, 23

"To me, the very least of all saints, this grace was given, to preach to the Gentiles the unfathomable riches of Christ, and to bring to light what is the administration of the mystery which for ages has been hidden in God, who created all things; in order that the manifold wisdom of God might now be made known *through the church* to the rulers and the authorities in the heavenly places. This was in accordance with the eternal purpose which He carried out (formed) in Christ Jesus our Lord, in whom we have boldness

and confident access through faith in Him."
Eph. 3:8-12

"He is also head of the body, the church; and
He is the beginning, the first-born from the
dead; *so that He Himself might come to have
first place in everything.* For it was the
Father's good pleasure for *all the fullness to
dwell in Him,* and through Him to reconcile
all things to Himself, having made peace
through the blood of His cross; through Him,
I say, whether things on earth or things in
heaven." Col. 1:18-20

" . . . a renewal in which there is no distinc-
tion between Greek and Jew, circumcised
and uncircumcised, barbarian, Scythian,
slave and freeman, but *Christ is all, and in
all.*" Col. 3:11

These scriptures, along with many more, show us God's
eternal purpose. Simply stated, it is to sum up all things in
Christ. God has a Person, a Man, who is to be the Center of
all things. This Person is His Son. His goal is to have this
Person be enlarged so that He fills the universe with
Himself. He is to be the all-comprehending and all-inclu-
sive One. He is to be all-encompassing and all-sufficient.
He is to be the All in all! All things are to be filled with Him
and He is to be the total equation of all things. God's goal
is that His Son would be the fullness of all realms. Yes, He
wants the Lordship and Headship of Christ to reign
supreme, but it is much more than that. All things are to be

in Him, and all things are to be filled by and with Him, that is, with His life. "He who descended is Himself also He who ascended far above all the heavens, *that He might fill all things*." Eph. 4:10

Do you see the issues here? He is to have the preeminence in all things. The issues are *filling, fullness*, and *all*. The *fullness* of Christ must be expressed throughout the universe and *all* that He is must be seen everywhere. He is to be the *All* in you and the *All* in me. He is to be the All in all of us! The life, love, character, and power of Christ are to permeate every inch of this universe. He is to be the beginning, the end, and everything in between. He is to be the Center *and* the Circumference. He is to be the end all and be all at all times and at all places. This is God's glorious will and purpose.

Of course, it is not enough just for us to know that this is God's purpose. The very purpose itself demands that we come progressively into a growing knowledge of the fullness of Christ Himself. Paul said that it pleased the Father to reveal His Son in him and this revelation was the basis for the gospel he preached. (Gal. 1:15, 16) We are to attain to the knowledge of the Son of God, to a mature Man, to the measure of the stature which belongs to the fullness of Christ. (Eph. 4:13)

God is going to fulfill His purpose by developing a Man. This Man is to grow into maturity so that the measure of His stature is the fullness of Christ. Now let's take a look at how God is going to accomplish this great goal.

CHAPTER TWO

THE VESSEL OF GOD'S PURPOSE

"I pray that the eyes of your heart may be
enlightened, so that you may know what is
the hope of His calling, what are the riches of
the glory of His inheritance *in the saints*, and
what is the surpassing greatness of His power
toward us who believe. These are in accordance with the working of the strength of His
might which He brought about *in Christ*,
when He raised Him from the dead, and seated Him at the right hand in the heavenly
places, far above all rule and authority and
power and dominion, and every name that is
named, not only in this age, but also in the one
to come.

And He put all things in subjection under His
feet, and gave Him as head over all things *to
the church*, which is His body, *the fullness of
Him* Who fills *all in all*." Eph. 1:18:23

We must now move on to take a look at God's method and means of fulfilling His eternal purpose. As we look at this vessel we must always keep in mind the goal of God. His purpose is the *fullness* of Christ. Anything that is deficient of fullness will come short of satisfying His purpose. He is not going to be satisfied with only a partial revealing and expression of Christ because He wants Christ to be the All. This means that all that Christ is will saturate all realms. Nothing less will do. God will not back down from this all encompassing objective. We need to grasp the gravity of His resolve in this matter.

God's Vessel – The Church

> ". . . and gave Him as head over all things to the church, which is His body, the fullness of Him who fills all in all." Eph. 1:22, 23

This passage of scripture has always boggled my mind. I have studied it, picked it apart, read it in many different translations, and it always comes out the same. The church is the *fullness* of Christ! Now the word for *fullness* in the original language is *"pleroma"* which literally means *completion*. Did you get that? Paul is saying here that the church is the *completion* of Christ! Is he stark raving mad? Can he be serious? How could he make such a bold declaration? It's because of his revelation into the purpose and mystery that was hidden in God before the ages.

You see, the church is the vehicle of God's eternal purpose. Now there is a good reason why Paul calls the church the body of Christ in this passage. Notice that he does not say that the church is *like the* body of Christ. No, the church *is* the actual body of Christ, the embodiment of His fullness, the actual completion of who He is. Isn't this tremendous?

Here again, the fullness of Christ is what is in view. But please notice with me that according to Paul, that fullness has already been deposited into a particular entity. That entity is the body of Christ. Can we get this into our spirits? The fullness is already there! The complete revelation, life, character, power, and Person of Jesus Christ have already been given to the church. The body contains His life and *all* that He is.

The Expression of Christ

So what's the hang-up? If the fullness of Christ is already deposited into the church, why hasn't His eternal purpose already been fulfilled? Why don't we see the universe radiating the glory of Christ? The answer is simple, yet agonizing. The fullness *must* have an expression. It's not enough to just have the fullness of Christ residing inside of a body. That body must express Him! That's why it is called a body. Does not your physical body express the life of the person who lives inside? Can you imagine a body that could not express the life of the person inside?

Let's think about this for a moment. Let's imagine that you, dear reader, are in this situation at this moment. Your body cannot express who you are in any way. You cannot smile. You cannot frown. You cannot roll your eyes; you cannot even open your eyes! In fact, you can't make any facial expressions at all. You cannot move your hands while you talk, and you definitely cannot talk! You cannot move one muscle in your body. In other words, you are like a statue except that you are a living person. You have life inside of you. You have a personality inside of you but with no way to express it, no outlet for this life and personality. From all outward appearances, you are not even alive.

I think you are getting my point. I am using the term "body" because the word "church" has been so badly abused. Since Paul tells us that the church *is* the body of Christ, I am on good scriptural grounds here. The term "body" is more difficult to misunderstand because everyone knows what a body is. Your human body is the vehicle of expression for your life.

Now remember that God's objective is to have the *fullness* of Christ expressed in all realms. His vehicle or vessel for that expression is the church, the body of Christ. The church is to fully express Him in every way. When we look at the church we should see Jesus Christ! We should see all of His thoughts, His feelings, and His will come out through the body. We should see His character, His power, and His authority expressed through the body. The fullness of Christ has been placed inside of the church, so the complete personality of Christ should be flowing out of the body.

Our Present Situation

So why don't we see this happening in the church today? Why don't we see the life and person of Jesus Christ flowing out of His body?

I believe the answer is two-fold. One problem is that we don't know how to get in touch with the life of Christ within us.

> ". . . that is, the mystery which has been hidden from the past ages and generations; but has now been manifested to His saints, to whom God willed to make known what is the riches of the glory of this mystery among the Gentiles, which is *Christ in you*, the hope of glory." Col. 1:26, 27

When Paul wrote this passage he said that Christ in you is the hope of glory. The word "you" there is in the plural. Christ in you (all) is what he is saying. He was speaking to the saints (plural). He was speaking to the body. Yes, of course, Christ is in you as an individual as well. But that is not what Paul is talking about here. He is saying that the hope of God's glory being made manifest on the earth is that Christ is in you (all). Christ is *in* the body.

Now, how do we get in touch with that life? How do we live by that life that is within us? How do we allow that life to flow out of the body?

The other problem is that the body of Christ is never given the freedom to express Him. In order for the body to express Christ, it must function freely. Paul had a lot to say about this. Every member of the body is to function if the fullness of Christ is to be expressed.

I will be taking a look at and addressing both of these problems throughout this book. First, let's take a brief look at how we got into this present situation.

CHAPTER THREE

WHAT HAPPENED TO THE CHURCH?

T he historical records of the church after the New Testament writings were completed are very sketchy to say the least. There are no reliable records between the death of the apostle John and the opening of the second century. When the records take up again in the second century, we see a church that is very different from the one seen in the New Testament. Men were grabbing for power and taking over regional territories, setting up a hierarchical system based on the principles of the world. By the fourth century, the simple pattern of the early church had been completely abandoned and the Roman church was in control. The ministry was put into the hands of a select few and something was set up which resembled the Old Testament Levitical priesthood, but also had many pagan customs added to it. The church became centralized in Rome with a man-made hierarchy of priests, bishops, cardinals, and pope. Of course, this was a chain-of-command, politically based system that has no foundation in scripture whatsoever. Man put Christ out of the church and put himself in charge. The church went into darkness and only a small remnant remained outside the institutional church to carry on the witness of God's testimony.

We need to realize that up to the third century the church was not popular! From the first persecution of Stephen in Jerusalem all the way up to the Roman emperor Constantine in 313 A.D., the church was almost continually under persecution of one sort or another. This kept the church on her toes spiritually. It was very costly to become a Christian in those days because you could possibly lose your job, house, or even your life! This tended to keep out the people who really weren't sincere about following Christ. Another important point is the fact that there were no church buildings of any kind until the third century. The believers mostly met in homes or (in times of severe persecution) in catacombs. Obviously this meant that their meetings were much smaller than many church meetings we have today. This will be important to remember as we progress.

The Church Becomes Popular

In 313 A.D., the Roman emperor Constantine issued his Edict of Toleration. This edict legalized Christianity. This, of course, meant the end of all persecution of the church. Christianity became more and more popular, church buildings started popping up all over, and the church became more like an organization than a body. The expression of Christ was being more and more suppressed.

For over a thousand years, the church went deeper and deeper into the world system and man-centeredness. It committed all sorts of gross sins in the name of God and played the harlot with the nations just like Israel did many times in the Old Testament. God called one man to speak out as a voice crying in the wilderness.

On October 31, 1517, a German monk by the name of Martin Luther took a hammer and some nails and tacked up his ninety-five statements on the door of the church in Wittenburg, Germany. This paper contained ninety-five reasons why the Roman Catholic Church and the Pope were wrong. You can imagine the stir that made! Within four weeks, all of Christendom had heard about the little monk's bold statements. Many began to discover that what he said was true according to the Bible and a major revolt began against the Roman church.

Martin Luther taught that all believers have the right to read and understand the scriptures for themselves. He translated the bible into German so that the common people could read it. He also taught that we are not saved by the church or by our actions, but only by grace through faith in the finished work of Christ on the cross. Of course, this was a great advance toward the restoration of the true church. It opened the way for all of the people to read the Bible and begin to hear from God for themselves.

Even though this "reformation" was a great step forward, the church was still far from being reformed or restored to its original splendor. Because many of the reformers and the people after them did not follow the Spirit, Christianity became a very divided and splintered group. Many new organizations, called denominations, began to come forth, each of them rallying around a certain leader or reformer. We see Lutherans, Presbyterians, Episcopalians, Anglicans, Baptists, and later, Methodists as well. Many other denominations formed after that, all with their very own "special truth or revelation" that they emphasized. So even though good things came out of the reformation, many things were still rejected or carried over from the Roman church. Even though the Bible was put into the hands of the believers, the ministry was not. What was actually needed was a complete abandonment of the organized church system and a restoration of the New Testament church. Instead, the reformers were mainly concerned with reforming the Roman Catholic Church and not with a return to primitive Christianity. The reformation was one of theology *not* practice! The priesthood of all believers was *not* restored to the church! The same clergy/laity system was still used. The only thing that changed was the names of the clergymen. Instead of being called priests, bishops, cardinals, and popes; now they were called pastors, ministers, parsons, preachers, and reverends! The system remained intact, only the names were changed to protect the guilty! It was still only a select group that ministered to God and man, taught the Bible and ministered the sacraments. This has pretty much remained the same right up to the present day.

CHAPTER FOUR

THE RISE OF THE CLERGY

One of the most destructive concepts and systems ever perpetrated upon believers is the idea of a separate class of believers who would be the "ministers" as opposed to the rest of the believers who would just be the people or "laity."

The clergy/laity concept and practice is one of those things that we never really stop to question. Is the concept of a professional clergy founded upon the scriptures? Where did this system come from? Is there a "caste" system within the church? Is it God's plan to send a man away to a seminary for four years, license and ordain him, and then pay him a salary to be the "Pastor" of a church? If there are professional Christians then doesn't it stand to reason that there would be amateur ones as well? Are not these questions crying out to you to be answered?

Origins of the Clerical System

The first thing we need to ask ourselves is: where did the professional clergy system come from? Does the New Testament teach and establish a professional order of ministers who are set aside to do the work of the ministry such as preaching and teaching, baptisms, ordination of other ministers, the Lord's Supper, weddings, funerals, counseling, and such? Did a church in the first century ever hire one of these men and pay them a salary to be the "Minister" for their congregation? The answer is an unequivocal "NO!" You will not find anything like our present day clergy system anywhere in the New Testament. It just doesn't exist. What you find instead is a body of believers who *all* minister to one another. What you find is a "priesthood of all believers." The whole body functions, not just a select few. Is this not in keeping with the eternal purpose? God wants His Christ to be the All in *all*. So, of course, it only makes sense that all believers would minister Christ. The fullness of Christ must be expressed, and that fullness is in the *body*, not a separated, elite class of believers. *All* have Christ in them, so *all* should be expressing that Christ.

Unfortunately, the clergy/laity system has all but destroyed every member functioning within the church. All functioning is now reserved for the "Pastor" and perhaps the worship or song leader. The rest of the "laity" has been reduced to a mere audience with perhaps the exception of the songs. In some more "progressive" churches there is some time set aside in the service when the people are allowed to share. What? The body of Christ being "allowed" to share? Every Spirit born believer has a divine right to function in the gatherings of the church!

Now I am not saying here that there isn't a legitimate place in the church for ministry and leadership. However, that leadership is nothing like we see prevalent today among the churches. Paul told us in I Cor. 12 that all members of the body have a ministry and function. Those ministries and functions are different for each one according to our calling. We are not all called to the same function, but we are all called to function. We were never called to be spectators!

Towards the end of the first century the churches were all run by the brothers and sisters under the headship of Jesus Christ. Some of the churches had elders but they were "shepherds" of the flock and only lead by example as brothers among brothers. There was no clergy or pastorate as we see it today. But where did this come from?

The Origins of One Man Ministry

At the beginning of the second century there was a man that began pushing for one-man rulership in each church. His name was Ignatius of Antioch. He taught that the "office" of bishop was different than that of elder and that each church should have a bishop who is "over" the elders. He taught that the bishop had absolute power over the congregation and the elders. The bishop was to perform the Christian "sacraments" of communion, baptisms, marriages, and preach sermons. This system came to take hold in most churches by the middle of the second century.

Cyprian of Carthage came along in the third century to do even more damage to the priesthood of all believers. He was a former pagan orator and brought many of his pagan ideas into the church. He was responsible for bringing back the Old Testament system of priests, temples, altars, and sacrifices. Bishops now came to be known as "priests" and were accepted as the representatives of God and anyone who questioned them would be opposing God Himself! This, of course, even struck a deeper blow to the priesthood of all believers.

But the question is; why did the churches allow this to take place? I believe that the present day clergy/laity system came about because of one root problem within the church. There are many symptomatic reasons that have been given for the rise of the clergy system, such as the grasping of men for power and prominence, the induction of the world system's methods, a misinterpretation of the Old Testament priesthood, and the installation of the Aaronic priesthood into the New Covenant. Even though we will be examining these things, none of them are the root cause of the rise of the clergy.

There is one single reason why any erroneous practices or doctrines come into the church. It's because the church has abandoned the centrality and supremacy of the Lord Jesus Christ! When this happens, the church becomes weak because the light of His life has all but been put out. The Spirit is grieved, and the church becomes vulnerable to the influence of the world, the flesh, and the evil one. At this point, the purpose of God is being frustrated because the church can no longer freely express Christ.

The Priesthood of a New Creation

This book is dedicated to the goal of helping you to see the need for the restoration of the priesthood of all believers. There are many reasons why the present day church is not expressing the fullness of Christ, but this is definitely one of the big ones. We are now going to take a panoramic view of priesthood in the scriptures. We need to understand the difference between the Old Covenant priesthood and the New Covenant priesthood.

CHAPTER FIVE

WHO IS MELCHIZEDEK?

T he first mention of any priest in the Bible is found in the book of Genesis, chapter fourteen and verses eighteen through twenty-four. This is the story of Melchizedek the king of Salem. There is much meaning behind this story of Abraham and Melchizedek. Let's see what God has for us in this story.

Melchizedek – Type of the New Priesthood

First of all, we must realize that the Old Testament is full of symbols and types that foreshadow spiritual truth in the New Testament. This story of Melchizedek and Abraham is one such type. It speaks of Jesus Christ, who is our High Priest, and the relationship and ministry of the church through the priesthood of all believers. Melchizedek is a type of the New Testament priesthood through Christ. It is important to notice that Melchizedek was a priest before the Aaronic/Levitical priesthood under the Law of Moses. Hebrews, chapter seven clearly states that Melchizedek was not after the order of Levi, because Levi did not even exist at the time! His priesthood was not under the law because it is an eternal priesthood based on the resurrection power of the Holy Spirit. Therefore, Melchizedek represents for us God's full thought concerning His eternal purpose.

There are several interesting things about Melchizedek that we need to look at:

He is a king and a priest. He is the only man known to be both a king and a priest in the Old Testament. Of course, this shows Christ as the King of kings and our High Priest. It also speaks of the church as being kings and priests unto God.

> "To Him who loved us and washed us from our sins in His own blood, and has made us kings and priests to His God and Father, to Him be glory and dominion forever and ever! Amen!" Rev. 1:6

God has called us to be *both* kings and priests. Our kingship speaks of our governmental authority in Christ, and our priesthood speaks of our ministry in Christ. Though right now we are "kings-in-training," the Word clearly tells us that if we overcome, we shall also reign with Him.

> "To him who overcomes, I will grant to sit with Me on My throne, as I also overcame and sat down with My Father on His throne." Rev. 3:21

Our ministry and position as kings and priests is eternal and God is going to have us co-rule the universe ministering to both God and man as priests. I don't know about you, but that sounds really exciting to me! God wants to prepare us for our eternal ministries by on-the-job training right now!

He is the king of Salem. Salem is the ancient name for the city of Jerusalem. Jerusalem means peace in Hebrew. Melchizedek was the king of peace. Does this sound familiar? Obviously, this is a type of Christ who is the *Prince of Peace*. This also speaks of our rest in Christ. He said, "I will give you *rest* unto your souls."

Jerusalem is the holy city, the city of David, and is referred to as the city of God in many places in scripture. In Revelation, Chapter 21, we see a picture painted for us of a new city, the New Jerusalem, built by God Himself (Heb. 11:10) and there is no need for any sun or moon because the Lord God and the Lamb are its light. In Revelation 21:10 it says that the New Jerusalem descends out of heaven from God. The scripture here is definitely not speaking of heaven, but rather, a city that comes down to earth *out of* heaven. In verse nine, we find out what this city really is: the bride, the Lamb's wife. Who is the Lamb if not Christ? Who is the bride and wife of Christ? The church! We know this to be true because Paul clearly ties Christ and the church to the husband and wife in Ephesians, chapter 5.

He brings out bread and wine for Abraham. This is a clear picture of the New Covenant meal, which we call the Lord's Supper or communion. Since Melchizedek is a type of Christ and since we (the church) are all children of Abraham by faith (Rom. 4:16), this speaks to us of Christ having the covenant meal with His church.

He pronounced a blessing upon Abraham. In Genesis 14:19,20 we have the blessing that Melchizedek pronounced upon Abraham. In the New Testament we have a similar blessing:

> "Blessed be the God and Father of our Lord Jesus Christ, who has blessed us with every spiritual blessing in the heavenly places in Christ, just as He chose us in Him before the foundation of the world, that we should be holy and without blame before Him in love, having predestined us to adoption as sons by Jesus Christ to Himself, according to the good pleasure of His will, to the praise of the glory of His grace, by which He has made us accepted in the Beloved."
> Ephesians 1:3-6

God has given us *every* spiritual blessing in Christ already! He has given us access to the heavenly realms by placing His life in our spirits. In the priesthood of all believers, we discover that those blessings are in us as well as in our brothers and sisters. We can discover the blessings that God has given us but have never uncovered because they are hidden in the members of the Body of Christ. God has given us many blessings, which are resident within each and every believer. The problem is that these blessings are not allowed to come out because of wrong practices and structures in the churches. As we study the scriptures with an open heart, we shall see that Christ is like a great prism, who reflects the glory of God. When the Light of God is reflected by this prism it is then divided into different colors and projected for all to see; a beautiful rainbow! Right now we are only seeing one or two colors, but God is in the process of restoring the complete rainbow.

<u>Melchizedekian priesthood totally different from Levitical.</u> In Hebrews 7:11-28, we see that the order of Melchizedek is completely different from the order of Aaron. The power behind Aaron's priesthood is the Law. The power behind Melchizedek's is an endless life. The order of Melchizedek is a clear Old Testament type of the New Testament priesthood of Christ and the church. This priesthood is based upon the power of the resurrection of Jesus Christ! It is not based upon laws, traditions, rules, and regulations. It is based upon the life of the Spirit as taught by Paul in the letter to the Galatians. We cannot live out our priesthood in the flesh. It can only happen as we yield ourselves to God by following the promptings of His Spirit. We can only learn to function in our priestly ministry in the power of the Holy Spirit. We have His life dwelling within us. Now we need to learn how to live by that life instead of our own human life. This is why we have so many immature believers today. I would say that at least 99% of our churches in America function as a show rather than a body. You have an audience, and you have a performer. The congregation is an audience instead of a functioning body of priests who are *all* ministering to God and to one another. Since the pastor does most of the ministry, the saints never really learn to hear the voice of the Spirit because they really don't need to, that pastor can do it for them!

Melchizedekian priesthood is eternal.

> "You are a priest forever, according to the
> order of Melchizedek." Heb. 7:17

Here the writer of Hebrews is quoting from Psalm 110:4 to
show us that the priesthood of Christ and the church is eternal as typified in Melchizedek. In verse three, he tells us
that this Melchizedek has no record of father or mother or
of his life at all! It also says that he remains a priest continually. The Levitical priesthood was only temporary. The
priesthood according to Melchizedek is eternal and fulfills
God's thought for His purpose. Only an eternal priesthood
could do this. Since the Father's purpose is to fill all things
with Christ, He would need a priesthood that was based
upon the life of His beloved Son. We do not know whether
Melchizedek was an actual person or whether this was a
pre-incarnate appearance of the Lord Jesus Christ Himself.
That is not really the point. The point is that the New
Testament priesthood of Christ and the church is not pat-
terned after the Aaronic/Levitical priesthood. It is true that
there are many insights that we can gain by studying the
Levitical priesthood, which also is a type or shadow of the
new priesthood in Christ. We must, however, realize that
the priesthood underwent a major change as we see
revealed to us in Hebrews, chapter seven. In order to fully
understand God's original intention for the priesthood, we
need to go back and take a look at the priesthood and how
it related to the nation of Israel.

CHAPTER SIX

GOD'S PRIESTLY NATION

T he first mention of a *priestly nation* in the bible is found in Exodus 19:5, 6:

> "Now therefore, if you will indeed obey My voice and keep My covenant, then you shall be a special treasure to Me above all people; for all the earth is Mine. And you shall be to Me a kingdom of priests and a holy nation."

A Nation of Priests

The language here is very clear. God wanted the *whole* nation of Israel to be a kingdom of priests unto Him. Notice that this was *before* the selection of the tribe of Levi and the sons of Aaron as priests. God's original intention was that *all* of the children of Israel would be priests, not just a select few. God wanted a holy nation that would show forth His glory to all creation, for all the earth is His. This would be a nation among nations; a model or prototype to show the world what living for the one true God could be like. This is because God always thinks in the corporate. Even when He calls individuals, it is always in relationship to the corporate. Abraham was an individual who was called by God, but within the one man was a whole nation. This was the Seed of Abraham.

God thinks in the corporate because He *is* corporate. He is a community of three Persons; Father, Son, and Holy Spirit. When He created man, He created him to be in His image, that is, corporate. This is why He said, "Let *Us* make man in *Our* image." (Gen. 1:26)

The priesthood speaks of ministry to God and man. Priests are ministers. Therefore, what God wanted from Israel was a whole nation of ministers! They would minister to God, to one another, and to the nations around them. They would manifest the authority, power, and character of Almighty God Himself! This was God's vision. This was God's goal and plan for the nation of Israel. Let's see how Israel responded to God's call.

Since God wanted all of the people to be priests, it's clear that He wanted to draw near and communicate to all of them, not just Moses. Tragically, in the very next chapter of Exodus, we see that the people were afraid and did not want the responsibility of ministry to God:

> "Now all the people witnessed the thunderings, the lightning flashes, the sound of the trumpet, and the mountain smoking; and when the people saw it, they trembled and stood afar off.

> Then they said to Moses, "You speak with us,
> and we will hear; but let not God speak with
> us, lest we die." And Moses said to the peo-
> ple; "Do not fear; for God has come to test
> you, and that His fear may be before you, so
> that you may not sin." So the people stood
> afar off, but Moses drew near the thick dark-
> ness where God was." Exodus 20:18-21

Unfortunately, the children of Israel did not receive God's
call on their lives. They wanted God to speak to them
through Moses and not directly to them. This is because they
did not want the responsibility of living out separated, holy
lives that would be a testimony to the world. They wanted to
follow God, but not utterly and completely to the point of
giving up sinful behavior and living consecrated lives, which
is a requirement for the priesthood. They did not want the
responsibility of ministry to which God was calling them.
Instead they asked Moses to take that responsibility for them
and be a mediator between them and God. This, of course,
was not God's plan and desire for them. He wanted the
whole nation to take up the call of priesthood. He wanted all
of the children of Israel to be ministers to Him, to one another, and to the nations. This was the heart desire or will of
God for the nation of Israel. Obviously, they rejected His
plan so God instituted an alternative plan to take care of the
needs of ministry to the people.

Levitical Priesthood

In Exodus, chapter 28, we see what God did to solve this
problem. He called one tribe out of the twelve tribes of Israel

to be set aside for the purpose of the priesthood. Since the whole nation would not be priests, God thought that maybe one tribe out of twelve might be willing. This was the tribe of Levi. Aaron and his sons were chosen to become the first order of priests unto God. Actually, as we saw earlier, Melchizedek's priesthood was the first. God designed special garments for them to wear and had special duties for them to perform. They were to offer sacrifices for the sins of the people. In short, they were to minister to God and the people. This priesthood never really seemed to accomplish much and it seemed that there were always problems from within. Just a few chapters later, in Exodus 32, we see Aaron (the high priest) making a golden calf for the people to worship! Of course, this was the natural course of things. When man refuses to obey God and wants a system, God will allow it, but it will never bear lasting fruit. It will always end up in devastation, confusion, and spiritual barrenness. God's answer is never a system but rather a *Person* — the *Person* of His beloved Son.

This order (the Levitical order) remained in operation until the death, burial, resurrection, and ascension of the Lord Jesus Christ. Even though it was a spiritually dead institution, it was still in operation until that time. When Christ came, He instituted a new order of priests, one ordered after the priesthood of Melchizedek.

The Corporate Melchizedek

Jesus Christ came to restore God's original intention and pattern for the priesthood: a whole nation of priests. Remember that first priest named Melchizedek? He was a model or prototype of what God wanted His priestly nation to be like. In other words: God wanted a corporate Melchizdek!

"The Lord has sworn and will not relent; You are a priest forever according to the order of Melchizdek." Psalm 110:4

Jesus came to establish a new kingdom of priests after the order of Melchizdek. In Hebrews 7:11-16, God tells us that this new priesthood is not according to the fleshly commandment (law of Moses), but rather based upon the power of an endless life. This new priesthood is based upon the life and power of God, not rules and regulations and man-made traditions. By Jesus' death on the cross, a new way was opened up for man to once again enjoy complete and unrestricted fellowship with God. Now man could approach the throne of God boldly (Hebrews 10:19-22) and enter into the very presence of God. The great barrier of sin was dealt with on the cross, now those who received this gift from God could enter in.

Now God could finally have His priesthood, which He desired way back before Moses and the children of Israel. His eternal purpose could now be brought back on course and He could get the eternal priesthood He wanted. Now He could have priests who could truly minister to Him and to one another because of the life that dwelled within them. They could serve Him because now they could intimately know the One who dwells within them. All this, of course, was made possible by the sacrifice of Jesus on the cross. Now God could have His priesthood after the order of Melchizdek.

"Coming to Him as to a living stone, rejected indeed by men, but chosen by God and precious, you also, as living stones, are being built up a spiritual house, *a holy priesthood*, to offer up spiritual sacrifices acceptable to God through Jesus Christ. But you are a chosen generation, *a royal priesthood*, a holy nation. His own special people, that you may proclaim the praises of Him who called you out of darkness into His marvelous light."
I Pet. 2:5, 9

God has called us, the church, to be His new priesthood, set apart and consecrated to be a glory to Him before the whole earth. A holy nation that would show the world what God is like and how much He loves them. This priesthood is now to be designed the way God originally intended with the nation of Israel except that now it would be much more glorious because of the New Covenant made possible by Jesus Christ. In other words:

The church is called out by God to be a nation of priests who minister to and for God!

All believers are priests and are called to minister.

"To Him who loved us and washed us from our sins in His own blood, and has made us *kings and priests* to His God and Father, to Him be glory and dominion forever and ever. Amen." Rev. 1:5b, 6

> "And they sang a new song, saying: You are
> worthy to take the scroll, and to open its
> seals; for You were slain. And have
> redeemed us to God by your blood. Out of
> every tribe and tongue and people and nation,
> and have made us *kings and priests* to our
> God; and we shall reign on the earth."
> Rev. 5:9, 10

The language is clear. The scriptures say that we, the church,
are a holy nation. We *are* a royal priesthood. It is already an
established fact. We *are* all priests unto our God! This is
exactly what God wanted and this is what He got in the early
New Testament believers. The church we see in the New
Testament was in full operation of this priesthood, as we
shall see in later chapters.

The Community of Priests

Please notice with me that Peter tells us that we are a royal
priesthood, not just a bunch of individual priests. The word
"priest*hood*" means a priestly "fraternity" or brotherhood.
Clearly, the scriptures are speaking of a *society* or *community* of priests. We have almost completely lost this in the
church today. We mostly view the church as a "place" to go
to learn about God, similar to going to a school or classroom.
The church is a building or a meeting that we *go to*. We don't
think of the church as a community of priests. Church is just
something we *attend* once or twice a week.

But that's not the "priesthood" we see in the New Testament.
There, we see a community or society of people who share

their lives in common. There, we see a "brotherhood" of those who take care of one another and really do practice the divine love that their Lord spoke about. That same Lord lived with such a group of people for the last three or four years of His life. This little *community* followed Him everywhere He went. They walked together, and ate together, and He was the Center of it all. He taught them as they walked along the road or floated across a lake. They experienced *Him* together! On the day of Pentecost, the twelve began to share the same life they had experienced for those three years with Jesus. Now the priesthood had grown to over three thousand and they began to live as a *community* of priests. They shared their lives in common, breaking their bread together daily from house to house. This was a family, a brotherhood, a community that shared the same mind, heart, and soul.

Think about the terminology that is used to describe the church in the New Testament.

She is Described as a Family

Her members are called brothers and sisters. God is their Father and they are all children in His household. In Paul's letter he calls the believers brothers and sisters. Of course, most of us today have a warped idea of what this means because all of our natural families are dysfunctional. But a family lives together, works together, cares for one another, and so forth.

She is Described as a Body

This is the most common term used by Paul. He calls the church the "Body of Christ." Do the parts of your human body only get together once or twice per week for a meeting? Let's hope not! "For even as the body is one and yet has many members, and all the members of the body, though they are many, are one body, *so also is Christ.*" I Cor. 12:12

She is Described as a Temple

The church is described as a temple made up of living stones. This speaks of God's dwelling, His continual presence within His people. We are the dwelling place of God. Christ dwells within the spirit of each individual believer, and even more so in us corporately. The living stones have all been placed into the temple by the Holy Spirit and live together as one to provide a dwelling place for God!

She is Described as a Bride

The relationship between Christ and the church is beautifully described in romantic terms for us by Paul in Ephesians, chapter 5. He describes the marriage union as a picture of Christ and the church. He even ties in the story of Adam and Eve with Christ and the church when he quotes from Genesis in verse thirty-one.

There are other terms used to describe the church in the New Testament but these are the main ones. All descriptions have to do with community of people sharing a common life; the life of Christ.

I have asked many Christians why they go to church and these are the kinds of answers that I have received.

To be spiritually fed – These believers view the church as being a feeding station or restaurant. They are always concerned about their own spiritual growth.

To learn about God – These believers view the church as a classroom. Their spiritual education is of the utmost importance. They are usually very big on studying the bible and filling their heads with "spiritual" concepts and principles.

To worship God – This reason sounds very high and lofty at first. However, when you discover that worship is something that is to be lived out all the time, and that Jesus said that we worship in our spirits, not in this place or that place, it loses validity. What these people are really saying is that they go to church to feel good. They will only go to a church if the "worship" is good. They are looking for a certain feeling that the singing will produce. It's kind of like a drug. Get your shot to feel good the rest of the week!

To get blessed or receive ministry – These believers view the church as a hospital more than any thing else. They always have needs and want prayer for their many needs. Or perhaps they are looking for guidance, a "word" from God, a healing, or a miracle.

To obey God – This is possibly the saddest reason of all. This believer doesn't really have a reason to go to church other than to obey that famous verse in Hebrews about not forsaking the assembling of yourselves together. He has no vision, no revelation, no passion for God's eternal purpose whatsoever. He just wants to make sure God doesn't get mad at him!

This covers most of the main reasons why Christians go to church. Now let's compare our list of descriptions of the church with the list of reasons to go to church.

They do not fit together at all, do they?

The way that we view the church has nothing to do with the way that God views the church! How does the idea of a feeding station, classroom, hospital, pharmacy, or "bless me" club fit into the descriptions used in the New Testament? They just plain don't!

We have reduced the vessel for God's eternal purpose down to a building, or a meeting, that we attend once or twice a week. What a shame! She is to be the living, breathing, glorious expression of the fullness of Christ! She is to be the full time priesthood who lives by the power of an indestructible life!

CHAPTER SEVEN

THE HEADSHIP OF JESUS CHRIST

There are two great principles of leadership in the New Testament: servanthood and the headship of Christ. First we will look at the headship of Christ.

Only One Head

The scriptures clearly teach that there is only one head of the church: Jesus Christ.

> "And He put all things under His feet, and gave Him to be the head over all things to the church." Ephesians 1:22

> "For the husband is the *head* of the wife, as also Christ is the head of the church; and He is the Savior of the body." Ephesians 5:23

> "And He is the head of the body, the church, who is the beginning, the first born from the dead, that in all things He may have the pre-eminence." Colossians 1:18

Jesus Christ is without question, the head of the church.

There is no other head and He does not share His headship with anyone. God is very particular in His use of words. He never wastes words or mixes up meanings between them. He says what He means and means what He says. The head is the part of the body that controls, directs, communicates, and makes decisions for the rest of the body. The head is in charge! The head is supposed to lead the body. Whoever heard of a body that did whatever it wanted to instead of listening to the head? The modern day church, in general, is not being directed by the head but by other parts of the body instead. In most churches around the world today, Jesus Christ is only a "figure" head and not the real head. Oh sure, everyone says and teaches that He is the head, but in actual practice, a man, or a group of men, is in charge of the church. Either that or the church may take a vote on decisions like a democracy. In any case, Jesus is not the actual ruler, but only a figure head or pretend-head like the queen of England. As we know, the prime minister and the Parliament are the actual rulers of England; the queen is only a figure head and is there for show only. We have made Jesus Christ a figure head and have put men in His place of real, practical headship. This all has to do with government.

Forms of Government

As we just saw in the scriptures, Jesus Christ is the one and only head of the church. This form of government is called a Theocracy. In simple terms, this means, God rules. He is the only head and king and ruler of His church. Unfortunately, this form of government is not being practiced in the churches of today. Instead, we have borrowed from the world several different types of government, which we use in practically all our churches. The three main forms are: democracy, oligarchy, and autocracy. All other forms of government are a slight variation or combination of these three. A democracy is a government in which the people all vote to make decisions. The majority vote wins. Part of the church has adopted this form and called it the congregational churches. An oligarchy is a government in which a group of men are in charge and make the decisions. Many churches today have a board of elders that make all the decisions for the church. An autocracy is where one man is in control as in the case of a dictatorship or monarchy. Many churches today have one man in control, usually called the Pastor. None of these forms of government is a Theocracy. None of these are scriptural. None of these are what God ever intended. People have always tried to set up their own kingdoms and systems of government instead of letting God rule over them directly. A good example of this is found in I Samuel, chapter eight. God had set up a system of judges over Israel who were there only to decide and preside over disputes. God wanted to rule over the people directly as their king. They looked at the other nations and saw that they had *human* kings and they wanted the same thing for their own nation. Samuel was upset and grieved over the requests of the people but God told him that it was He that they were rejecting from being king over them. God let the people have their human king and it ended in disaster for many generations.

The modern day concept of a Pastor has no foundation in the scriptures whatsoever! The early churches did not have a Pastor over each one of them like we do today. They would never have done such a thing. To do so would have meant substituting the headship of Jesus Christ with a man. The whole concept of the modern Pastor was taken from the pagan religions and brought into the church by Constantine in the third century. Pastor, you are actually usurping the headship of Jesus Christ in His church.

Practicing His Headship

So, right about now I bet you're asking how do we practice the headship of Christ in the church? The only way in which we can put to practice the headship of Christ is in the Holy Spirit. There's no way that we can do it in the natural. God designed it that way, so that we would fail every time we tried another way. The only way in which we can implement the headship of Christ is through the priesthood of all believers: Jesus being our High Priest (or Head). The decision-making responsibilities lie squarely on the shoulders of Jesus and the believers: not on a professional clergy system. Let's take a look at how the early church practiced the headship of Christ.

The church of the New Testament practiced a principle that I call the threefold witness.

The threefold witness is: 1) the Holy Spirit, 2) the elders, and 3) the whole church. These three must agree as to what the mind of the Lord is before a decision or direction is taken in the church. We can probably see this the clearest in the Jerusalem church's decision in Acts, chapter fifteen. The key verses are:

"Then it pleased the apostles and elders, with the whole church, to send chosen men of their own company to Antioch with Paul and Barnabas, namely, Judas who was also named Barnabas, and Silas, leading men among the brethren." Acts 15:22

"For it seemed good to the Holy Spirit, and to us, to lay upon you no greater burden than these necessary things." Acts 15:28

Notice with me, that in verse twenty-eight, it seemed good to the Holy Spirit and to *us*, the "us" here is obviously a reference to verse twenty-two which includes the leaders of the church together with the whole church. The leaders of the church did not make this decision by themselves. There is no mention of a vote being taken with the majority winning. The leaders, *together with the whole church*, had to find out what was pleasing to the Lord by the Spirit. So how did they do it? There can only be one way.

"Assuredly, I say to you, whatever you bind on earth will be bound in heaven, and whatever you loose on earth will be loosed in heaven. Again I say to you that if two of you agree on earth concerning anything that they ask, it will be done for them by my Father in heaven. For where two or three are gathered together in MY name, I am there in the midst of them." Matt. 18:18-20

> "Now in the church that was in Antioch there were certain prophets and teachers: Barnabas, Simeon who was call Niger, Lucius of Cyrene, Manaen who had been brought up with Herod the tetrarch, and Saul. As they ministered to the Lord and fasted, the Holy Spirit said, "Now separate to Me Barnabas and Saul for the work to which I have called them." Then having fasted and prayed and laid their hands on them, they sent them away." Acts 13:1-3

Here is the key. The early church fasted and prayed and then God, the Holy Spirit, spoke to them as to what they should do. They came together in the name of Jesus. They came together in agreement. Because of this, Jesus, by His Holy Spirit, was in their midst. In this atmosphere of worship and prayer, God could speak to His people and direct the affairs of the church. Jesus could be the actual head of the church! As the church gathered together and ministered to the Lord (worship), God would speak to His people. This "speaking" could have been an inner witness in the hearts of the believers, or an operation of the gift of prophecy through one or more of the saints. Whatever vehicle God used to communicate, it was clear that the whole church agreed as to what the mind of the Lord was for that particular matter. They didn't take a vote. They didn't form a committee. They didn't call the main office to see what they should do. I take that back, they did call the main office (in heaven – through prayer) to find out what they should do. They simply came together in the name of the Lord, in agreement, and worshipped and prayed and God spoke. That's how it's supposed to be done; every believer seeking the Lord to get the mind of Christ in unity with his brethren; every believer taking on the responsibility of hearing from God for the decisions made in the church.

Maturity through Responsibility

Can you imagine how strong and fast believers would grow if this were put into practice in the churches of today? Every believer would quickly learn to hear from God for himself, instead of stumbling around in the dark or learning to depend upon other believers all their lives. Their spiritual senses would rapidly develop to be able to discern good from evil (Heb. 5:14). Or in other words, they would be able to discern what is God and what is not God. They would be able to digest solid food, which is direct revelation, and not just be spoon-fed like spiritual babes. They would learn to walk in the Spirit and live in the Spirit every day of their lives. Does this sound impossible? Does this sound too good to be true? Believe me, dear saint, it's not!

We have two levels of Christians in the modern day church:

Level One: This is the professional Christian, the clergy, the "ministers." They are more devoted, committed, and mature than the rest of the church. They are more "spiritual." Their job is to hear from God for the rest of the church. This is what we pay them for.

Level Two: This is the "laity" or ordinary believers. They are the audience in this show. The clergy *give* ministry and they *receive* it. They don't have to be as devoted as level one. They are like the members of a great club. They don't have to produce, only attend the meetings and pay the dues!

Can't you see how destructive and unbiblical this system is? God expects *all* believers to grow into maturity. He expects *all* believers to produce fruit and minister in the power of the Holy Spirit.

Here again, this is in keeping with God's eternal purpose. He wants the fullness of Christ to be displayed. This includes the authority (headship) of His Son, Christ being the *All* in *all*.

CHAPTER EIGHT

SERVANTS AS LEADERS

There is a principle that our Lord taught which is the foundation for all spiritual leadership. If we do not practice this principle, we will surely end up with man's egocentric kingdom being built, instead of the kingdom of God. We will be building our house upon the shifting sand.

The Principle

> "So He said to them, "You will indeed drink My cup, and be baptized with the baptism that I am baptized with; but to sit on My right hand and on My left is not Mine to give, but it is for those for whom it is prepared by My Father."
>
> And when the ten heard it, they were moved with indignation against the two brothers.
>
> But Jesus called them to Himself and said; "You know that the rulers of the Gentiles lord it over them, and those who are great

exercise authority over them. *Yet it shall not be so among you*; but whoever desires to become great among you, let him be your servant. And whoever desires to be first among you, let him be your slave – just as the Son of Man did not come to be served, but to serve, and to give His life a ransom for many." Matthew 20:23-28

"But you, do not be called Rabbi'; for One is your Teacher, and you are all brethren. Do not call anyone on earth your father; for One is your Father, He who is in heaven. And do not be called leaders; for One is your Leader, the Christ. But he who is greatest among you shall be your servant. And whoever exalts himself will be humbled; and he who humbles himself will be exalted."
Matthew 23:8-12

This is the principle of servanthood that Jesus taught. It says that in order to be the greatest, you must become the least. In order to become first, you must become the last. Humility is the key, and you can't fake it with God! You have to really put yourself last in order to succeed in God's kingdom. This is another principle that is being ignored in the modern church.

The leaders in today's church seem to be the least humble of all the saints. It looks like they're the ones who are lording it over the flock and reaching for power and recognition. Most pastors today want everyone in their church to call them "Pastor." Well first of all, it's not their church. The church belongs to Jesus Christ and the saints. Secondly, we just read the passage of scripture where Jesus tells us very clearly not to call anyone father or rabbi or teacher. What's the difference if we call him Pastor? Don't you realize that a rabbi is a Jewish pastor? If Jesus had said Pastor, the disciples would not have understood. The only Pastors at that time were the rabbis. The point is that Jesus is not into titles because titles puff men up with pride. We don't need titles to show our leaders respect and if they are demanding our respect then they have a *real* problem with pride already! Remember, *all* believers are ministers; therefore, all believers must become servants. There's no room for pride here.

This is an extremely important principle for leaders of the church to follow. There is such a thing as true spiritual leadership in the church of Jesus Christ. In order to hold true to their calling, they must *always* practice this principle of servanthood. They must live by the life of Christ who came to serve, not to be served. They must be broken men who have been severely dealt with by the cross.

For our purposes in this book, we don't need to go into a detailed look at church leaders, however, I think it would serve us well to take a brief overview.

First Century Leaders

In the early church there were only two functions of leadership ever mentioned: elders and deacons. Within these two functions God has provided everything necessary for leadership in the church. Elders are the spiritual leaders of the church. They are to watch over (oversee) the flock. They are to protect the flock. Please see Acts 20:28-38 for references. According to Ephesians 4:11, 12 they are to equip and train believers to do the work of the ministry. They are *not* to be "the ministers" for the congregation. They are *not* to do all the ministry while the believers sit down and soak it all in. Their ministry is to equip the saints to do *their* ministry. It's important to point out here that there is no record of any church having elders in the beginning. Paul and Barnabas went back to the churches in Galatia about 1 – 2 years later to "point out" or acknowledge elders. Some churches seem to have no indication of ever getting elders such as Corinth. Paul's letters to that church were written several years after its birth and yet no elders are mentioned in his letter in spite of the fact that they had many problems. This, of course, does not prove that they did not have elders at the time. But it does show that if they did have elders, Paul certainly did not feel it necessary to write to these elders concerning the problems in the church. And that church had lots of problems! Why didn't Paul write this letter to the elders asking them to address these problems? There can be only two possibilities. Either they didn't have any elders yet (even though this church was by now five years old!), or Paul didn't seem to think it was necessary to address this letter to them. Now let's think about this for a moment. If the elders were the ones that made decisions and solved problems in the church, why wouldn't Paul direct this letter to *them*? Instead he directs his letter to all of the brothers and sisters in the church.

"Paul, called as an apostle of Jesus Christ by
the will of God, and Sosthenes our brother,
to the church of God which is at Corinth, to

those who have been sanctified in Christ
Jesus, saints by calling, with all who in every
place call upon the name of our Lord Jesus
Christ, their Lord and ours . . ." I Cor. 1:1,2

This, of course, was not the only church that had problems.
Yet Paul addresses his letters to the whole church. Why?
Isn't it obvious to you? It's simply because Paul considered
the responsibility of the church to be in the hands of all the
brothers and sisters! He wrote to them because he expected
them to handle it. Paul's concept was that the whole church
was responsible for dealing with these problems.

Elders are not to make the decisions for the church as we
have already seen. The elders, together with the whole
church are to seek God for His will in full agreement as to
what that will is. The elders must never try to take this
away from the church. The elders are simply older brethren
who are more mature and experienced and can "watch
over" things. They are not *over* the saints, they are *among*
them. In Matt. 18, Jesus taught that if your brother offends
you, after taking witnesses, you are to take it before the
church, not the elders. In Revelation 2 and 3, Jesus
addresses His remarks to the seven *churches*, not the seven
elders! You see, Jesus said that He is the vine and we are
the branches. Obviously, He was speaking of a grape vine.
On a grape vine, all of the branches connect directly to the
main vine.

Leadership in the early church was always plural. It was
always elders (plural), never elder or pastor (singular).
Nowhere do we see that there was one man who was in

charge in any local church, because it would take away the practical headship of Christ over His church. Elders and deacons were always plural in every church. There was no "senior elder or pastor" who was ultimately in charge. Jesus was the actual Head of every church with the leaders all working together in unity. Remember, they only wanted to be servants and not possess some position of authority over others. There is no indication in the New Testament records that any leader ever held an official position in the church. Paul and his co-workers never placed elders into an official position. They simply "acknowledged" them. That's what the word literally means in the Greek, not "appointed," but acknowledged or recognized. They just recognized what God had already done. This was not done in every church, but only in a few areas such as Galatia, Ephesus and Crete. Elders were not "special," they were just some older brothers. Their motivation for everything was the exaltation and magnification of Jesus Christ as Lord of all. The elders and deacons were simply priests among priests who were there to train and develop the other believer's ministries and watch over the church. Every priest understood that they were responsible to function. They knew who they were in Christ.

CHAPTER NINE

YOU ARE A PRIEST

"You are a priest forever, according to the order of Melchizedek." Psalm 110:4

One of the major problems in the church today is the fact that most Christians don't know who they are in Christ. They really have no idea why they are here, what they are supposed to be doing or where they are going! This lack of identity and direction is a very real problem in the church today. We are having a spiritual identity crisis!

I believe there are two main contributing factors in our identity problem in the church: low self-esteem and lack of knowledge. Let's take a look at self-esteem first.

The Identity of the Believer

It doesn't take a genius to look around and discover that just about everyone in this world has an identity problem. This is one of the resulting effects on the human soul of a sin stained world system. We have almost all been abused by someone at one time or another. This abuse may have come as verbal, mental, sexual, emotional, or physical. It may have come through parents, relatives, schoolmates, friends, husband/wife or even pastor. This is why the world has such an identity problem. People just don't seem to know who they are. You may have heard the phrase, "I need to find myself." Well they wouldn't need to "find" themselves if they weren't lost! People are always looking for someone else to identify with. Just look how people identify themselves with famous singers, movie stars, and athletes. Many people even imitate their idols by dressing like them or copying some other trait. We love to make idols out of people. We wish that we could be just like our favorite celebrities because we've actually convinced ourselves that they have it made. If we could just be like them we would be happy. What a bunch of lies! The fact is that we are very insecure within ourselves and feel like we don't measure up. We know that we should learn to be ourselves; the problem is that we don't know what our "self" is! Even if we did discover who we are, we probably wouldn't want to be that person anyhow! This is the way it is in a world without God. It will continue this way until a person comes to Christ. The real tragedy is when a person does come to the Lord and still has this problem. The even greater tragedy is that most Christians *do* have this problem!

Forgiveness

The two steps to resolving the problem of low self-esteem are forgiveness and identity. First of all, we must forgive all of those people who have hurt us in our past. If there is any unforgiveness or bitterness in our hearts, it will literally eat us up from the inside out. Take an inventory (in your mind, or perhaps even write it down) of all the people who have said or done something that has hurt you. One by one verbally speak forth forgiveness to each one. Pray for God's blessing to be poured out on that person and for God to forgive them as well (remember what Jesus prayed on the cross?). As you do this, God will release you from the chains of bitterness that have held you down.

Identity

The second step in overcoming low self-esteem is realizing your identity in Christ. First of all, let me say that the only way that you can find out who you are is through and in Christ. Becoming your own best friend won't help. Dianetics won't help. Psychology won't help. Self-realization won't help. The only place where you can find yourself is in Christ. There is no other way. He is the way, the truth, and the life. He is the one who created you and apart from Him you will never find out who you are. He designed it that way. Apart from Him you can do nothing; but through Him you can do all things.

Dear reader, you need to understand that you have a spirit, a soul, and a body. When you were born again, the Godhead came to live inside of your spirit. This is incredible! The God of all creation actually lives inside of you. This means that you can now live by means of the same life that Christ lived by; the very life of God, the Father! You need to come to terms with this awesome fact and learn to turn to your Lord who is within.

You need to know three things:
> *Who* you are
> *Where* you are
> *What* you have

The following is a list of scriptural references as to who and what you are in Christ:

Child of God	I John 3:1-3
Priest of God	I Peter 2:9
Temple of God	I Corinthians 6:19, 20
New Creation	II Corinthians 5:17
Friend of God	John 15:15
Servant of God	Isaiah 54:17
Saint (Holy One)	I Corinthians 1:2
Chosen One	Colossians 3:12
God's Possession	I Corinthians 6:20
Bride of Christ	II Corinthians 11:2
Soldier	Ephesians 6:10-17
Conqueror	Romans 8:35-37
Heir with Christ	Romans 8:16, 17
Ambassador	II Corinthians 5:20

Dear believer, when you were born again you were *actually* born into God's eternal Family. This is not just a theory or belief. It is an established fact. According to John 3, you were actually born of the Spirit into God's family. You are a child of God. The mighty God who created the universe is your Father. He wanted you to be a part of His family so bad that He sent His only begotten Son to die for your sin so that you could enter into His kingdom. You are not an orphan. You are not a reject. You are not a failure. You are a child of the King of kings.

Because you are a child of God this means that you are part of His great family, the church. Your identity is not only based upon your individual relationship to God but is intricately woven together with the community of believers. You are a member of the body of Christ. Your true identity can only be discovered as you begin to relate to other brothers and sisters in the Lord. Your experience in Christ is not to be a solitary vocation. The early church lived out their lives together, in one accord, in daily fellowship, sharing their meals as well as their lives.

Another thing that you need to realize is that you are not a mistake. God had you designed and formed in detail in His mind before the foundations of the world.

> "For You have formed my inward parts; You have covered me in my mother's womb. I will praise You for I am fearfully and wonderfully made; Marvelous are Your works, and that my soul knows very well. My frame was not hidden from You, when I was made in secret, and skillfully wrought in the lowest parts of the earth. Your eyes saw my substance, being yet unformed. And in Your book they all were written, the days fashioned for me, when as yet there were none of them."
> Psalm 139: 13-16

Another thing that you need to know is that *you are accepted in the beloved.* By God's grace He has made you acceptable. Before the cross you were not acceptable because of your sin. But now you have been saved by grace through faith in the atoning sacrifice of Jesus Christ on the cross.

"Just as He chose us in Him before the foundation of the world, that we should be holy and without blame before Him in love, having predestined us to adoption as sons by Jesus Christ to Himself, according to the good pleasure of His will, to the praise of the glory of His grace, *by which He has made us accepted in the beloved.*" Ephesians 1:4-6

Knowing *where* you are is also very important in understanding your identity.

"For you died, and your life is hidden *with Christ in God.*" Colossians 3:3

"But God, who is rich in mercy, because of His great love which He loved us, even when we were dead in trespasses, made us alive together *with Christ* (by grace you have been saved), and raised us up together, and made us sit *together* in the heavenly places *in Christ Jesus.*" Ephesians 2:4-6

The position, which we now occupy, is *in* Christ. We are in Him and with Him where He is. We are seated with Him in the heavenly places. This means that our legal position is in Christ. According to Romans, we died with Christ and have been raised up together with Him. Because of this, the victory, which is Christ's, is ours also! *Positionally*, we have already overcome the world, the devil, and the flesh; experientially, we are still walking it out. Being *in* Christ means that we share in everything that is His. The exception to this is of course His deity. We do *not* share in that. Everything else is ours because we are in Christ. This brings us to the realization of *what we have in Christ*. We have all of His fullness!

> "And He put all things under His feet, and gave Him to be head over all things to the church, which is His body, *the fullness of Him* who fills all in all." Ephesians 1:22, 23

Since we have His fullness this includes all authority *in His name*. The scripture says that all authority in heaven and earth has been given to the Lord Jesus Christ. Since we are *in* Christ, this means that this authority has been given to us as well. Of course this does not mean that we can do anything we want with this authority. It is *His* authority and *His* power and can only be used in *His* name. This authority includes all authority over the devil (see Luke 10:19). We have the authority in the Name of Jesus to bind, cast out, and pull down all the strongholds of the enemy.

Since we are in Christ, the following scripture applies to each one of us individually:

> "You are a priest forever, according to the order of Melchizedek." Psalm 110:4

That's right, dear believer, *you are a priest!* This means that you have been called and anointed by the Holy Spirit to minister as a priest to God and to man. Your place in the church is very important! If you do not function in your priestly ministry, the church will be missing a very important, vital part of the work of the Holy Spirit on the earth! You are needed!

Scripturally speaking, there is no such thing as a clergy/laity system in the church. In the New Testament church all believers were ministers. All were not leaders; but all were ministers. The priesthood of all believers means that every believer has spiritual gifts and ministries and that God intends for everyone to exercise these gifts within and without the church. When the believers/priests are given the freedom to do this in the church gatherings, their self-esteem will greatly improve. Actually it won't be self-esteem at all but rather *Christ-esteem*! Jesus said that we must deny ourselves, pick up our cross, and follow Him. In other words, abandon yourself. Forget yourself. Lose your life (self-life) in order to gain eternal life. It's a fantastic blessing to be used by God to minister to someone else. It causes you to come out of yourself in order to bless someone who is in need. This is an outworking of eternal love. Only eternal love can conquer the self-esteem problem. This is because we discover our own worth in relation to God and His people. There is a freedom and a release that God gives us when we serve (minister to) someone else. The church has been suppressed for 1700 years. It's time to liberate God's people to do the work of the ministry! We need to understand what the functions of a priest are in order to do this.

CHAPTER TEN

PRIESTLY FUNCTIONS

"For every high priest is appointed to offer both gifts and sacrifices." Hebrews 8:3a

Thus is the twofold function of the new priesthood. New Testament priests are to offer both gifts and sacrifices. First, let's take a look at the ministry of offering sacrifices.

"Therefore by Him let us continually offer the sacrifice of praise to God, that is, the fruit of our lips, giving thanks to His name." Hebrews 13:15

"I appeal to you therefore, brethren, by the mercies of God, to present your bodies as a living sacrifice, holy and acceptable to God, *which is your spiritual worship*." Romans 12:1

Spiritual Sacrifices

Our first and foremost ministry as priests is to offer up praise and worship to our God. This is our first priority. This is the ultimate service, function, responsibility, privilege and blessing. There is no greater ministry than to minister to God in worship. Do you realize what I am saying? We can actually minister to the God of all creation! That's right, my friend, worship is ministry to God. Let us never forget this. Our first and primary ministry as priests is to God.

Do we put this ministry to God first in the modern day church? We say that we do. We even have what we call "worship services." But do these meetings really put God in the center? Don't they rather put the ministry to man as the main focal point? Don't they rather put the comfort, convenience, interest, and needs of man before those of God? Think about it. Do we try to get the mind of God for what He wants to do in the meeting or do we just stick to "business as usual" with our programs and schedules? What is the actual focal point of the meeting? Isn't it the teaching or the communion? You see, these things are important but they focus on what Christ can do or has done *for* us. Worship, on the other hand, focuses on *who God is*. True worship is completely God-centered with no stain of man in it. It brings everything into proper perspective because when you worship you realize and confess how great God is and how small you really are! You express your love to God and exalt and magnify Him. You lift *Him* up and glorify *Him*. This is a work of death to our own ego, pride, and self-centeredness. Yes, worship is indeed ministry to God, but guess what? When we worship Him in spirit and truth, when we minister to Him, He loves to minister right back to us! Worship is our sacrifice, which we offer up to God.

New Perspective Needed

First of all, let me say that by and large, our concepts of worship are somewhat twisted. We commonly think of worship as you and I bowing down to a most high and holy God. Now, of course, our God is the most high and holy and should be honored and revered. But the actual word "worship" means something quite different.

The word "worship" in the original language literally means: *to move towards a kiss*. That's right, we are talking romance here. Your God is a romantic! He wants to have an *intimate* relationship with you. Worship is the *act* of your intimacy with God. It's the act of you coming and loving Him with all that you are. It's also the act of you *receiving* His love for you. This is an act of the will and is done by faith. You receive His divine love, and then give that same love back to Him. This can only be done with your spirit. And this can only be done in His Spirit.

> "God is spirit, and those who worship Him
> must worship in spirit and truth." John 4:24

Of course, this is not just to be an occasional act once a week or something. Our whole lives are to be an act of worship. That's why Paul would say that we should present our bodies (and all that is in them) a living sacrifice to Him. (Romans 12:1) This is not only an individual matter, but even more so a corporate matter. We are dealing here with a God who wants romance. He is a passionate God who wants an intimate relationship with His bride.

Now we are getting at the very heart of the priesthood of all believers. Remember God's purpose? That the fullness of Christ would be expressed in all realms, that He would be the All in all. In order for this to happen, His life must freely flow among the members of the body. Organic, first century-styled church life is simply the life of Christ flowing in, among, and through His people. In other words, church life is Christ-life. Or put even more simply and directly; the church *is* Christ!

The Oneness of Christ and the Church

Now I realize that there are those of you out there right now that are screaming "blasphemy!" But that's only because you have a twisted concept or definition of the church. To say that the church is Christ would only be heresy if you believed that the church is *people*. And surely you and I are not Christ! But is it possible that we have missed something that's right there in the New Testament?

> "Saul, Saul, why are you persecuting *Me*?"
> Acts 9:46

> "For even as the body is one and yet has many members, and all the members of the body, though they are many, are one body, *so also is Christ*." I Cor. 12:12

> "Now I mean this, that each one of you is saying, "I am of Paul," and "I of Apollo," and "I of Cephas," and "I of Christ." Has *Christ* been divided?" I Cor. 1:12-13a

". . . to whom God willed to make known
what is the riches of glory of this mystery
among the Gentiles, which is *Christ in you,*
the hope of glory . . ." Col. 1:27

You see, the church is not people. The church is Christ *in*
people. The part of Christ that is in you, *that* is the church!
God has placed His Son in you, that Person, *that* life in you
and *that* life in me is the church. When the parts come
together, there is Christ. This is something that is completely spiritual and comes from the heavenly realm. However,
God's purpose is that this spiritual life would have a practical expression in this realm. In other words, He wants to be
made visible. He wants to have an image in the physical
realm, a corporate image. Christ came as a man to make this
possible.

Worship – Communion with God

Believe it or not, this all has to do with worship. Worship is
not something we just do occasionally when we come
together at a church meeting. Worship is a life. Worship is
our romance with God. I am speaking of a deeply intimate
relationship and exchange, an interchange of divine life. We
must learn how to live by His life and to allow it to flow out
of us; otherwise the body just won't work. How can we
express the life of Christ corporately if we don't have it
flowing in our own lives? We need to learn how to fellowship with Him in our spirits. We need to learn how to take
Christ as our food and to live by Him each day.

"As the living Father sent Me, and I live because of the Father, so he who eats Me, he also shall live because of Me." John 6:57

Spiritual Gifts

Before we begin our discussion of spiritual gifts, there is something that I want you to realize and keep in mind. When Paul speaks about spiritual gifts and/or ministries, he always does so in the context of the body. Spiritual gifts belong to the body, they are not individual possessions. Not only that, but spiritual fruit and gifts are the natural result of spiritual life. Your face just naturally grows ears, eyes, nose and a mouth. You don't have to work at that, it just happens because you have life. It happens organically. You don't need to study the gifts or worry about what your gifts are. Just get to know the Lord and His church and the rest will follow. If life is flowing in the body, then all the gifts and callings of God will just naturally appear. We don't need to make a big fuss about gifts. God's purpose is to express the fullness of Christ, not to bring attention to the gifts themselves. The reason that I am briefly mentioning spiritual gifts here is so that you will realize that God's will is that all believers function as priests and ministers to one another and the world.

As I believe we all know, God is not only concerned with our ministry to Him, but also our ministry to one another and to the nations. In worship, we will receive the insight, revelation, and power we need in order to minister to the needs of other people. We read about this happening to the early church on the day of Pentecost. In Acts, Chapter 2, we read that it was when the believers were together in one accord, worshipping, fasting, and praying that the Holy Spirit came upon them. God poured out His Spirit because they humbled themselves and obeyed Him. From this moment forward we see the early church moving out in great authority and power. Each believer/priest had their own gifts and ministries, which God gave them, and were using those gifts as led by the Holy Spirit.

Every believer has spiritual gifts that God has given them. These gifts are given by God to be used by the believer in order to minister to others. Remember, priests are ministers. Therefore, God, through the Holy Spirit, distributes gifts, or tools for ministry, to each believer just as He wills. This is clearly taught in I Cor. 12, Romans 12, Eph. 4, and many other places in the scriptures. Let's combine the lists of gifts and ministries given in these scriptures and see what we get.

ROMANS 12	I COR. 12	EPH. 4
prophecy	word of wisdom	apostles
teaching	word of knowledge	prophets
exhortation	faith	evangelists
giving	healing	pastors/teachers
leading	miracles	
showing mercy	discerning of spirits	
	different tongues	
	interpretation of tongues	

I am not going to describe to you how each gift should look or function. It is not for us to say. Preachers have gotten into a lot of trouble by pigeonholing believers and spiritual gifts or ministries. Our God is a God of endless variety. These gifts can be expressed in an infinite number of ways. God will not be bound or limited by our narrow descriptions and definitions. God is looking for the unsearchable riches of Christ to be expressed through the body. That can take many shapes and forms. The important thing is that this expression is Christ and not some man-made machine concocted by the religion of men.

Please understand that these are spiritual gifts, not natural talents! Sure, God will use the natural talents that He gave you for His kingdom, but God is not limited to these only. He will give you gifts in order to do things you have never done before and would never be able to do in the natural. These are *supernatural* gifts God gives to every believer/priest. Why does He give us these gifts? To use, of course! It is the job of every leader in the church to develop these gifts in the believers so that the ministry of Christ would be expressed. This is the task of equipping the saints spoken of in Eph. 4:12. Now I need to ask this very crucial question: Are you leaders out there developing and equipping the priests to do their ministries, or are you doing all the ministry yourselves? Are you running the whole show or are you allowing the priests to all have their part in the work of the ministry? Remember, God has called us *all* to be priests and to thus minister.

Gifts Belong to the Body

One very important thing that we need to realize is that God has called us to be priests *together*. We are not just a bunch of priests all doing our own things, we are a *priesthood*. We are a community of priests. We are the body of Christ.

"From whom the *whole* body, joined and knit together by what *every* joint supplies, according to the effective working by which *every* part does its share, causes growth of the body for the edifying of itself in love." Ephesians 4:16

"For in fact the body is not one member but *many*. If the foot should say, "Because I am not a hand, I am not of the body," is it therefore not of the body? If the whole body were an eye, where would be the hearing? If the whole were hearing, where would be the smelling? But now God has set the members each one of them, in the body just as He pleased. And if they were all one member, where would the body be? But now indeed there are *many* members, yet one body. And the eye cannot say to the hand, "I have no need of you;" nor again the head to the feet, "I have no need of you." No, much rather, those members of the body which seem to be weaker are necessary. And those members of the body which we think to be less honorable, on these we bestow greater honor; and our unpresentable parts have greater modesty, but our presentable parts have no need. But God composed the body, having given greater honor to that part which lacks it, that there should be no schism in the body, but that the members should have the same care for one another. And if one member suffers, all the members suffer with it; or if one member is honored, all the members rejoice with it. Now you are the body of Christ, and members individually." I Cor. 12:14-27

The Church, Which is His Body

This is definitely one of the most important illustrations of the church in the whole Bible. Paul is comparing the church of Jesus Christ to a human body. This illustration or example is extremely descriptive in nature and gives us a very beautiful picture of the practical operation of the church. Notice again that Paul does not say that we are *like* a body of Christ. He says, rather, that we *are the* body of Christ. This is tremendous! We are the actual body of Christ. He is the head and we are the body. Christ and the church are one. We are all members or parts or organs in that body, each with his or her own particular place and function. I Peter 2:5 says that we are living stones being built up into a spiritual house. We are not bricks. Bricks are all the same size, shape, composition, etc. Stones, on the other hand, are all individually different and unique. We, as the body of Christ, are all individuals yet we are all in the same body, living and working together in love. We are different, yet we are one. When one member suffers, we all suffer. When one member rejoices, we all rejoice. We share all things common, including our very lives! This is body life. This is the body of Christ. Every member is equally important and equally needed. No one or two members should hog the show. *All* members are to participate equally. Even though all members share the ministry, not all have the same function or operation of that ministry. God loves diversity and variety.

What would you call the problem if only part of your body were able to function? If only your right hand could move and function, what would the rest of your body be? *Paralyzed!* That is exactly the problem with the modern church. The body of Christ on earth today is paralyzed. Only a very small portion of the body is actually functioning to any degree. The rest of the body is simply sitting by frozen and unable to move. This is a very unhealthy situation. The church is not making any noticeable impact on the world today. We are in a spiritual coma! We need God to wake us up so that we can function in our proper place in the body. A few members are doing all the work for the rest of the body. The church is not a spectator's sport. The body of Christ calls for total participation of all members. Of course in order to see this happen, first of all, we need to change the way we think about the ministry. The leaders in the church need to move aside and let the *whole* body minister. Dear leader, if you really care about the church and the true pattern for the church, then you need to teach, train, and encourage all of the believers to participate in the ministry. Don't worry about *your* career! Your job is to equip the saints to do theirs. This will only happen as you step aside and let others carry the baton. Don't be afraid to let go. Trust in the Holy Spirit to move through the believers no matter how young they are in the Lord. Paul had elders in many churches after one year. It's God who does the work, not you.

Every Member Functioning in Love

Now we come to the most important aspect of all ministry.

It is no coincidence that right after I Cor. 12, the chapter on the gifts, ministries, and body of Christ, that we have Chapter 13, the chapter of eternal love. You see, without love, the whole ministry is just a bunch of noise. Talk is cheap. Love is the backbone of all true godly ministry, without it we only have a lot of religious activity. Of course we're talking about God's love, eternal love, perfect love. This perfect love casts out all fear. This love never fails. This love is what the world is starving for, and just think, we have this love in Jesus Christ! Jesus said that if we love one another, then the world would know that we are His disciples (John 13:34, 35). The early church really loved one another. They gave and shared all their possessions (Acts 4:32-37). They laid their lives down for the brethren (I John 3:16). They met together daily and prayed and worshipped and worked together constantly (Acts 2:46, 47). To them, church was not a place or a meeting. It was life itself. That is what I meant when I called it *church life*. That flow of life, love and fellowship was what gave the early church its power and strength. The community of believers depended upon one another and they always came through. If there was a need, it was met. This is the true ministry of Jesus Christ through His body. We desperately need a revelation of the body of Christ for today. Dear brother or sister, you need the other members of the body. There are no loners in the body of Christ. You need to be connected in fellowship to your brothers and sisters in Christ. This cannot happen in church meetings only. You need constant relationship and fellowship with the other members of the body. This is your life supply! You cannot be a separated part of the body. How will you get the blood and nutrients you need? You will soon die (spiritually) like a fish out of water. You need the body of Christ! You need the priesthood of Christ.

Please realize that *you* cannot love the brethren. It must be Christ in you. We all fail to love one another all of the time. It's only as you get to know Him and love Him that you will find yourself loving your brothers and sisters.

CHAPTER ELEVEN

PRIESTS TO THE NATIONS

The Testimony of the Church

When we, as the body of Christ, really learn to live by His life, then there will be fruit and the world will stand up and take notice. They are waiting for someone to show them the way. Notice that I said *show*. They need to not only *hear* the gospel; they need to *see* it in action. Like I said before, talk is cheap. The world wants to see a demonstration of God's love, not just a lot of talk with nothing to back it up. I believe people are finally beginning to see that this worldly system is falling apart very rapidly. The economy is going downhill fast. World governments are crumbling (including the U.S.) as people see the corruption in their leaders and lose confidence in them. Terrorism is everywhere. Drug lords and gangs have taken over the streets. The police are even corrupt from within. Abortion, infanticide, and euthanasia are increasing at alarming rates. Homosexuality is rampant and AIDS is spreading throughout the whole world. Pornography is everywhere and even entering our homes via cable TV, the Internet, and videos. Our educational system is falling apart and our children are more illiterate than ever. We are being taxed to death and many people can't even buy a home now. Where is it all going to end? What is the answer? Well, of course, you and I know that the answer is Jesus Christ. The problem is that the people of this world don't believe that because they don't see anything different about God's people! We're supposed to not only tell them the answer, but show them the answer by pointing to the church and saying: "This is the way it's supposed to be." The church is supposed to be an alternate society within society. Like a city set on a hill, the church is supposed to be a community of light which is working while the rest of society is failing. Isaiah 60:1-7 speaks about the nations coming to Zion because her light has come and the glory of the Lord is risen upon her. This is really exciting! If we build the church according to the pattern God gave us in the scriptures, with Christ as the Head, Center, and life, and we restore the priesthood of all believers, guess what will happen? The glory of the Lord will fill His temple once again and we will see the nations come to her. This brings us to the final aspect of our ministry as priests: our ministry to the nations or the world.

Remember what God's original plan was for Israel? Let's read it again.

> "Now therefore, if you will indeed obey My voice and keep My covenant, then you shall be a special treasure to Me above all people, for all the earth is Mine. And you shall be to Me a kingdom of priests and a holy nation."
> Exodus 19:5, 6

And also:

> "But you shall be named the Priests of the
> Lord, Men shall call you the Servants of our
> God, you shall eat the riches of the Gentiles,
> and in their glory you shall boast."
> Isaiah 61:6, 7

God has always wanted (and still does!) a holy, priestly nation that would stand out in the world as being special; a nation among nations, a holy nation in an unholy world. He wants a society of people who would shine forth as a bright light in a dark place or a watchtower or lighthouse on the edge of a dark and foggy sea. Jesus called the church a city set on a hill, the light of the world, and the salt of the earth.

God clearly wants His people to be a redeeming influence upon this world. He did not call us to change this world system. This world system, or cosmos, can never be changed or saved in any way. It's like a sinking ship and only the people can be saved from out of it. God did not call us to save this world. He called us to present the people of this world with a new "system" or order: the kingdom of God. In the kingdom of God, people must be born of the Spirit to see it and be willing to suffer tribulation to enter it (John 3:3; Acts 14:22). God is the supreme ruler in this kingdom. Jesus is the king. The subjects of the kingdom are His servants and they submit to Him. Their relationship however, is one of love and friendship as well as authority and submission. He is the Bridegroom and we are His Bride. Whether they know it or not, the people of this world need this relationship of the kingdom. It is our ministry as priests to present it to them in word and in deed. The problem is that when we go to minister to the nations, we leave a large part of our priestly ministry behind!

In Demonstration of Power

I have said before that what the world needs to see is a demonstration of the gospel, not just preaching. Paul practiced this principle in his own life.

> "For our gospel did not come to you in word only, *but also in power*, and in the Holy Spirit and in much assurance." I Thes. 1:5

> "And my speech and my preaching were not with persuasive words of human wisdom, but in demonstration of the Spirit and power." I Cor. 2:4

> "For the kingdom of God is not in word but in power." I Cor. 4:20

What Paul is saying here is that he didn't just tell people that "Jesus is Lord," he *showed* them! How did he show them? He showed them through the power of the Holy Spirit. How is the power of the Holy Spirit made manifest? Remember our look at I Cor. 12? It is through the gifts of the Spirit to the church that the power of Christ is made manifest. That's right; the gifts of the Spirit are not just for the church. The gifts are also to be used to minister to the world. Jesus did it. The apostles did it. The early believers did it. They all ministered to the unsaved by using the gifts of the Spirit and preaching in word and in power. There are many examples of this in the New Testament. We'll just take a look at a few of them in the ministry of Jesus and the early church.

Light and Salt to the World

In John 4:5-29, we have the account of Jesus with the Samaritan woman at the well. In His discussion with this woman, Jesus tells her that she has had five husbands and the man she's living with right now is not her husband. She said He must be a prophet; this was because there was no natural way that Jesus could have attained this knowledge. It was an operation of the supernatural gift of the word of knowledge, which is listed in I Cor. 12.

There are, of course, many instances in the life of Jesus when He used spiritual gifts. We see Him using the gifts of healing, miracles, prophecy, showing mercy, word of wisdom, discerning of spirits, faith, etc. These instances are easily found in the gospels and I'm sure we don't need to point them out. Of course, all of these instances when Jesus used the gifts were for unbelievers. Since Christ is *the* gift of the Holy Spirit, He was just sharing Himself with these people.

The early church also used spiritual gifts to minister to the unsaved. Here's a list of just a few:

Instance	Gift
Peter and John with the lame man	healing
Ananias and Sapphira, Peter	word of knowledge
The apostles	miracles
Philip in Samaria	healing, spirits

Cornelius' household	tongues
Antioch church (Acts 13:1)	prophecy
Paul (Acts 19:11)	miracles
Paul (Acts 16:16-18)	discerning of spirits

Please notice with me that in many of these accounts the spiritual gifts were used by God to minister to an unbeliever. Many times a healing or miracle would lead to the preaching of the gospel. This happened in the case of Peter and John at the Gate Beautiful. God used them to heal the lame man, and because of this, a crowd gathered and Peter preached with the result of many turning to the Lord. Today, it's usually only the evangelist at the evangelistic rally who used the gifts to bring in the unsaved. Why is this?

Hindrances

I believe there are a few main reasons why we don't use the spiritual gifts to reach the lost. One reason is that most of us aren't even used to operating in these gifts! If we are not functioning in the gifts regularly in the church, it will be very difficult to function properly in the gifts and minister to unbelievers. If the priesthood of the believer is working properly in a church, then the believers will continually be flowing in the gifts of the Holy Spirit. This "flow" will just naturally spill over into the believer's lives outside the church as well. Supernatural gifts should be an intricate part of the lifestyle of the believer, not just a few isolated incidences of manifestation. This flow of the gifts inside and outside of the church will occur if we learn to overcome one other obstacle.

Another reason why the gifts aren't used like this is simply because of fear, the fear of man. Of course, the enemy comes in and uses our fear to completely bind us from ministering to the lost. Since he is a defeated foe, there is nothing he can do to us unless we believe his lies. The early church prayed for boldness and for signs and wonders.

> "Now, Lord, look on their threats, and grant to Your servants that *with all boldness*, they may speak your word, by stretching out Your hand to heal, and that signs and wonders may be done through the name of Your holy servant Jesus." And when they had prayed, the place where they were assembled together was shaken; and they were all filled with the Holy Spirit, *and they spoke the word of God with boldness.*" Acts 4:29-31

The early church not only prayed for boldness, but also for signs and wonders to be done in the name of Jesus. We need to do the same! The following fictional scenes could be examples of testimonies being shared regularly in the church meetings.

You go to work today and one of your fellow workers gets a migraine headache. You've already shared Christ with this person, so he knows you are a Christian. Because you are used to ministering to people in need, you ask him if you can pray for him. He says yes, you lay your hands on him and pray. God heals him instantly and you have the blessed opportunity to lead him to the Lord.

At a wedding, you have a chance to talk to an old friend from high school. You both are engaging in the usual chit chat and finding out what the other person has been up to. Suddenly, in the midst of your thoughts, God begins to reveal to you that this person is desperately lonely and has seriously considered suicide on many occasions. This is an operation of the gift of the Spirit – a word of knowledge. You (because of praying for boldness) begin to share with this person their loneliness and depression and they are utterly astounded! "How did you know?" they ask. You share with them that Jesus knows all about it and that He loves him and died for him so that he doesn't have to be alone any more. You go on to share about how Christ actually lives within you and that you fellowship with Him all day long. He is always with you and in you and will never leave you. He is absolutely amazed and invites you over for dinner to hear more.

These are just two examples of what could be occurring all the time in the lives of true New Testament priests. God earnestly desires for this to happen and it will happen if the life of Christ is flowing in the church. Every priest needs the freedom to be able to minister in the gifts of the Holy Spirit to the church on a regular basis. How can we minister to the world in the power of the Holy Spirit if we can't even minister to one another?

The Greatest Sign

What is the greatest and most powerful sign we can show to the unbeliever? Is it tongues, healing, deliverance, prophecy, or miracles? No. The greatest sign is love. Jesus said that the world would know we are His disciples by the fact that we love one another. Paul said we could have all the gifts but if we do not have love then it's all worthless. That's really all the world is looking for; love. They don't care all that much about which group performs the most miracles or has the most healings. They are looking for love. Who is going to love them?

A New Commandment

Of course, there are two sides to every coin. The world needs to see the love we have for one another, and they need to see the love and acceptance we have for them. The problem is that they don't see either one of these coming from the "church." Why is this? Why can't we love one another? Why can't we love the world?

I know there are many reading this book right now who are thinking that I have totally lost it. You may be thinking that we *can* love one another because Jesus told us to do it. He would never command us to do something we could not do. Oh really? Then why did He give the law? Paul said that the purpose of the law was to show us our sin. In other words, *the purpose of the law is to show us that we can't obey it!* We have all failed to keep His law. We have all failed to be righteous and good. "We have *all* sinned and come short of God's glory."

The problem is that when we hear these words we think that they are about the unbeliever. After all, this is part of the "Roman Road" that we use to bring people to the Lord. This verse is talking about the unconverted, isn't it? No! This verse (Romans 3:23), and the rest of Romans, was written to the *church* in Rome! This is written to believers because this is exactly what they needed to hear. They (the believers in Rome) could not obey God!

Today, we tend to think that after we are saved, God somehow gives us the ability to obey Him. This is *not* what the New Testament teaches at all. Even believers fail to obey the law. No, *not one* is righteous. No, *not one* is good! Even after we are saved, we do not possess the ability to obey God.

So then why would Jesus give us a *new* commandment to love one another if we could not obey it? For the very reason that God gave us the "old" commandments; to show us that we cannot do it! The law never gave anyone life. The law can only be fulfilled by divine life, that is, God's own life. You cannot obey God by your own human life. Even Jesus Christ said that He could, of Himself, do nothing. The one man who actually did fulfill the law completely was the man who said He (in Himself) could do nothing! How is this possible? Because He did all that He did by the life of His Father within Him. It was the Father who did the work.

Only God can love your brothers and sisters and only God can love your neighbors. It's only as we learn to live by His life within us that these things will become a reality in the church again. As I have said throughout this book, the true priesthood of all believers can only become a reality by us allowing God's life to flow in us and through us.

Christ Centered Evangelism

I firmly believe that once we have true first century style

church life flowing in our midst, we will once again see true Christ centered evangelism. It will be evangelism that flows out of divine life, not some program, crusade, or system that is based on a set of scripture verses or memorized sermon. It will be outreach that quite naturally flows out of divine life with Christ as the center.

When believers live the church, then sharing, loving, and giving just organically happen. When the church is a *community*, then outsiders can see the loving and caring that is being shared and desire to belong to that kind of a family. Believers can share with non-believers about their own experiences with their Lord and the church.

When Christ is the center of everything, we can share our love for the Lord with someone and it will be filled *with Him* instead of things *about* Him. We will be sensitive to His Spirit to know when and how to speak. We will be able to discern where that person is coming from and how to minister to their present need. Not only that, but they will not be able to come in contact with us individually without coming in contact with the body. If they hang out with one person in the church then they will see the church because each one is so intimately involved with the life of the body. You will not need to invite that person "to church" because the church is your daily life and they will not be able to help but come in constant contact with the fellowship of saints.

What Comes First – Believing or Belonging?

Evangelism is no longer a program when the church is a community. His life must flow out. It's like the tree that must bear fruit because it is absolutely bursting forth with life. The overflow of life must go somewhere, so it explodes into these little pods on the ends of the branches. The pods (fruit) contain the seeds of life and drop off the branches in order to feed others. The fruit is just the natural consequence of life flowing through the tree. Divine life must be shared. The Father *must* share His life with the Son. And the Son *must* share His life with the Father through the Spirit. This is just the way that God is.

The "evangelical" concept of evangelism and conversion is that we must first make a "Gospel" presentation to the unbeliever such as the "Roman Road" or the "Four Spiritual Laws," and then lead them into a "sinners prayer" on the spot before they can be allowed to participate in the church. They must believe before they can belong. But is this the way that Christ "evangelized" the twelve disciples? Jesus traveled about the countryside of Galilee with an entourage of people who really didn't know Him yet. He included them in the "group" before they believed. It's hard to say when the disciples actually started to believe, but it's apparent that it happened gradually. The point is that Jesus accepted them into the group without them making a statement of faith, praying the sinner's prayer, or signing some oath or creed. If you carefully look through the gospel accounts, you will see that they gradually came to believe. Some of them, like Thomas, didn't even believe after seeing Him resurrected! So we can say that they belonged before they believed.

If we would just love and accept people for who they are and include them in the life of the church, then we would see them come to Christ. They would see Him through His body instead of some tele-evangelist or high pressure presentation. They would see His love and fellowship in reality being demonstrated before their eyes.

During the Middle Ages, the Celtic Christians in Ireland proved that this does work. They accepted people into the fellowship of their communities without demanding a confession of belief. "Seekers" often came to Christ in a matter of days or weeks as a result of participating in the life of the Christian community. We forget that our most powerful means of witness is the loving and caring within the church herself. But of course, if we don't have true church life flowing in our midst, then we really have nothing to bring the "seeker" into except a program or a meeting.

People are tired of being preached at or pressured into going to a "church" meeting. They need to see a life, the life of the body of Christ. They want to belong to a family that will love them and care for them with no strings attached. They need to see the brotherhood that is a priesthood with Jesus Christ as the High Priest!

CHAPTER TWELVE

THE GATHERING OF PRIESTS

In light of these principles of the priesthood that we've been learning, how is the church meeting supposed to operate? What things should be taking place there? Is the typical modern church meeting run in a scriptural manner? Let's examine these questions in the light of God's word.

New Mindset Needed

First of all, before we can truly understand what Paul and the other New Testament writers were attempting to communicate, we must completely change our way of thinking about the church. The church has added and changed and twisted things so out of shape since the first century that the only way in which we can clearly see is to start from scratch. What I mean by that is that we need to begin our understanding of church with a clean slate. We must erase all the preconceived ideas about what is necessary in church life. I know that it's difficult, but we need to look at the church in the scriptures as if we had no knowledge about church whatsoever! Let us come as little children being completely open to God's word as our only source of truth.

Apparently, the early church conducted different meetings for different purposes. Here are a few examples of recorded meetings and their functions.

1. Prayer   Acts 3:1; Acts 12:12
2. Teaching   Acts 19:9; Acts 20:7
3. Breaking bread   Acts 20:7; Acts 2:46

When the whole church came together it was quite a sight to behold! Our best description of this is given to us by Paul, in I Cor. 11-14. The breakdown of the subject matter for these chapters is as follows:

Chapter Eleven   The Lord's supper
Chapter Twelve   Spiritual gifts / Body life
Chapter Thirteen   Love
Chapter Fourteen   Prophecy/Tongues/Meetings

Since we have already covered chapters twelve and thirteen, let us now take a close look at chapters eleven and fourteen.

In chapter eleven, Paul teaches us about the Lord's Table or communion.

The Lord's Supper

The Lord's Supper or communion is discussed in I Cor. 11. This is something that the church has taken and twisted totally out of shape. The Roman Catholic Church has over emphasized it and the Protestant church as under emphasized it! The Roman church has taken the Lord's Supper and made it the central theme of the meetings, mingled together with the re-creation of the crucifixion which they call the "mass." They have 'deified' the bread and wine and take it literally to be the body and blood of Christ. The Protestants, on the other hand, have reduced the communion to a mere symbolic act, which is necessary (but why?) and really not very important. Most protestant churches only practice this once per month and most of the people really don't look forward to it or understand what it's all about. Obviously, if Jesus told us to do this in remembrance of Him, it must be important!

The problem is that most Christians don't really understand the full meaning and depth of the Lord's Table or communion. What we have done is taken it completely out of its natural context and made it into a ritual that is most unnatural and awkward. The reason that we have lost the meaning and depth of the supper is that we have not practiced it like Jesus and the early church did. Jesus didn't have a communion "service" with His disciples the night He was betrayed! He had the Passover meal with them. I am not implying by this that we should be having the Passover meal in church. What I am saying is that this was clearly a *meal*, not some crackers and grape juice! Jesus shared a full-on meal with His disciples.

The book of Acts also tells us that the early Christians broke bread together. Breaking bread was a term used to denote the regular meal, not a cultic ritual. To really understand why this is so important, we need to look at the most detailed account of the Lord's Supper in I Corinthians 11.

"For I received from the Lord that which I

> also delivered to you: that the Lord Jesus on
> the same night in which He was betrayed
> took bread; and when He had given thanks,
> He broke it and said, "Take eat; this is My
> body which is broken for you; do this in
> remembrance of Me." In the same manner
> He took the cup after *supper*, saying, "This
> cup is the new covenant in My blood. This
> do, as often as you drink it, in remembrance
> of Me." I Corinthians 11:23-25

In this passage, the word, supper, is *'deipnon'* in the Greek.
It literally means: a feast, dinner, supper, the chief meal of
the day, taken at or towards evening. It is a full-fledged
feast! Notice with me that in verse 25 it says that He took
the cup *after* supper. He passed out the bread before the
meal, and then passed the cup after the meal. What was
sandwiched in between was extremely important. We have
taken out the meat of what Jesus did here and now we're left
with two slices of bread! Now of course, the reason that
Paul is reciting what took place with Christ and the disciples is because he wants the Corinthian church to do the
same thing. Why in the world has the church separated the
breaking of the bread and the drinking of the cup from the
meal? This major alteration has deprived us of the true
meaning and experience of the Lord's Supper. Please let me
explain.

The Lord's Supper is a meal. It is not part of a meal. It is
not a cultic, ritualistic meal. It is simply a meal. This was
simply a customary meal in a Jewish home. The chief meal
of the day was always preceded with the breaking and dis-

tributing of bread. It was likewise common for the meal to be consummated with the drinking of wine with prayers of blessing being attached to both. The bread and the cup are not simply two ways to refer to the same thing: Jesus' death for our sins. He also says that this cup is the new *covenant* in My blood. This means that the meal not only signifies what Jesus did on the cross but also gives us an opportunity to partake of the great benefits that result from His death. This covenant means a new relationship with God and one another. This now brings us into view of the importance of the meal between the bread and the cup. During the meal itself we experience this new relationship as we eat and drink together as an expression of our unity as the body of Christ. This is tremendous! This meal actually cements the bond between us. Our sense of community is brought to new heights and we can enjoy the blessings of fellowship with God and man, which Christ obtained for us on the cross. At the close of the meal, when we drink of the cup, we celebrate the return of Christ and the coming Marriage Supper of the Lamb when Christ will be married to His Bride forever more!

Most believers only understand the outward, obvious meaning, which is the fact that it is a celebration and a remembrance of what Jesus did for us on Calvary. The bread and cup, of course, symbolize the body and blood of Jesus Christ, which was sacrificed for us on the cross for the forgiveness of our sins. This, of course, is very true and is definitely the most basic level of meaning of the Lord's Supper. However, this is not the complete meaning behind this blessed event. Again, we need to take a look at the New Testament to see what the early church believed and practiced regarding what Paul referred to as the Lord's Supper.

First of all, let me share that it is not my purpose here to give a detailed teaching on the Lord's Supper, but rather to fill us in on some of the missing parts and bring things into perspective. The first thing we need to bring into perspective is the importance of this event. Besides Jesus Himself, the early church also regarded this as a very important activity.

> "Now on the first day of the week, when the disciples came together to break bread, Paul, ready to depart the next day, spoke to them and continued his message until midnight." Acts 20:7

A Full Meal

It is clear from many other references in the book of Acts that breaking bread is referring to the Lord's Supper. In those days, sharing a meal or supper was referred to as breaking bread. Also notice that they came together to break bread. It seems that the main purpose of their gathering was to break bread, though teaching, obviously, was also included. In this instance it was Paul who spoke. For most believers today, it is merely a ritual, which is not very important and holds little excitement. I believe the reason for this is because it is not properly taught and practiced by the churches. What is this breaking of bread all about? Let's take a brief look at what the Lord wants us to experience in this blessed event.

"Behold, I stand at the door and knock. If anyone hears My voice and opens the door, I will come into him and dine with him, and he with Me." Rev. 3:20

This verse in Revelation is an invitation from the Lord Jesus Himself for us, His church, to open the door to fellowship and commune with Him. He says that He will dine with us, and we with Him. In Jewish culture, sharing a meal or breaking bread together is synonymous with fellowship. This is true even today in our culture. Usually, when we want to fellowship or have someone come to our home to get to know them, we do it over a meal. There is something about sharing a meal together that brings people together and opens the door for communication.

Clearly, Jesus desires to have intimate fellowship or communion with us in this meal, which He instituted. It's not just a ritual when we remember Him. It's a time when we, as a church, actually open the door to intimately fellowship with our Lord. It's a time for worship, reflection, repentance, and true two-way communication and adoration between us and the Lord Jesus. It's a time for us to celebrate our oneness in Christ.

"The cup of blessing which we bless, is it not the communion of the blood of Christ? The bread which we break, is it not the communion of the body of Christ? For we, being many, are *one* bread and *one* body; for we all partake of that *one* bread." I Cor. 10:16, 17

The One Bread

This scripture is rarely mentioned in connection with the Lord's Supper, yet is obviously referring to the supper of the Lord, or communion. This passage shines a different light and brings in another dimension to the supper. For through this we can now see that because of what Christ accomplished on the cross, we not only can have communion with Him, but also with each other. Remember I Cor. 12? We are the body of Christ. The one bread represents the fact that we are one body. This is why I believe the early Christians used one loaf of bread instead of many pieces. They called it breaking bread. How can you *break* bread if it's already broken into pieces? The one bread speaks of the oneness that we have with each other in Christ. Jesus took *one* bread and *one* cup and gave it to the disciples.

Why do we break the bread into tiny pieces beforehand and put the wine/juice into little cups? Are we afraid of communicating diseases to each other? Paul says that we won't get sick if we discern the Lord's body rightly. People were getting sick in Corinth because they were not "discerning" the body. They allowed many divisions to disturb their expression of the oneness of Christ. Oneness and fellowship are the keys here. This is a time for us to enjoy the blessed love that we can share in the fellowship of the saints. During this time we can minister to one another as well. We can go to another brother or sister and break bread with them and pray for them, sharing our individual love and concern. We don't have to make this into a dead ritual that is the same every time! Let's be flexible and creative and let the Holy Spirit lead in this activity as well as all others. This is not to be a solemn, depressing time. It should be a celebration of Christ and His body.

Prophesy One to Another

In I Corinthians 12, Paul speaks about the gifts of the Holy Spirit and body life. We have already looked at this, so we'll only mention it briefly now. Remember, Paul is instructing the believers in Corinth on how to conduct their meetings. He already spoke of the communion or Lord's Supper, now he speaks about spiritual gifts. Spiritual gifts are supposed to be a normal occurrence in church meetings. Of course, things can get out of hand and abuses can occur. This is the reason why Paul instructs the church in Corinth on the proper way to do things, decently and in order. Just because abuses can occur doesn't mean that we should stop using the gifts. Let's not throw out the baby with the bath water! Scripture clearly teaches that the gifts are to be used freely in all of the meetings of the church. This is an extremely important part of the priesthood of the believer and if it is not allowed to flow properly, major loss will occur in the local church. Remember, all believers are priests, and therefore all are ministers. The gifts of the Holy Spirit are the tools of ministry. You can't do the work right without the right tools.

Let's see what Paul had to say about this important subject.

> "Pursue love, and desire spiritual gifts, but especially that you may prophesy. For he who speaks in a tongue does not speak to men but to God, for no one understands him; however, in the spirit he speaks mysteries. But he who prophesies speaks edification and exhortation and comfort to men. He who speaks in a tongue edifies himself, but

he who prophesies edifies the church. I wish
you all spoke with tongues, but even more
that you prophesied; for he who prophesies
is greater than he who speaks with tongues,
unless he interprets, that the church may
receive edification." I Cor. 14:1-5

Apparently, Paul is telling us here that prophecy is the most
important gift for the church gathering. Note, he is not saying that tongues are unimportant. He is saying that *in the
church meetings* prophecy is more important because it edifies the whole church. What is prophecy anyway? Vines
Expository Dictionary of the New Testament defines it like
this:

"PROPHETEIA (Greek) signifies the speaking forth of the mind and counsel of God. It
is the forth telling of the will of God in the
past, present, and future. It is the declaration
of that which cannot be known by natural
means. It can include preaching and teaching inspired messages from God's word. It
ministers edification, exhortation, and comfort according to I Cor. 14:3."

Prophecy is a great tool to teach the believer how to hear
from God and move with the Holy Spirit. This is one of the
most important lessons for the believer. All believers need
to learn to hear from God for themselves. Prophecy is one
of the ways in which they learn this valuable lesson. As
they pray for someone in a meeting, they need to seek God
for what He might say to that person through them. Then

it's a matter of stepping out in faith in what you believe you are hearing God say to you. You will make mistakes, but that's OK, you learn by doing. Paul definitely places a priority on the gift of prophecy. Do we do the same today in our meetings? Of course, this can only happen in a meeting where the Holy Spirit is allowed to move through the various members of the body and the priesthood is allowed to function. If we are a Christ-centered people, then all gifts and ministry (including prophecy) will be Christ-centered as well. Any personal ministry that takes place will not be a man-centered, needs-centered, group therapy session, but rather a true Spirit born, Christ exalting, time of ministry to someone's needs. Christ is the supply for all our needs. He is the one who is to minister and be ministered to. Therefore, the way that church meetings are run is very important.

> "How is it then, brethren? Whenever you come together, each of you has a psalm, has a teaching, has a tongue, has a revelation, has an interpretation. Let all things be done for edification." I Cor. 14:26

> "For you can all prophesy one by one, that all may learn and all may be encouraged." I Cor. 14:31

Every Member Functioning

As you can surely see by now, the early church did not conduct meetings the way that we do today. In the modern day church, the meetings are dominated by one (or maybe two)

people. Every meeting is more or less the same with a pro-
grammed order or structure in mind. The teaching is the
most important part and everything else revolves around
that. Many pastors believe that the purpose of the worship
is to "set up" the meeting for the teaching! Usually there is
a predetermined schedule and time to end the meeting. The
typical modern church meetings will usually contain these
five elements: music/worship, announcements, offering,
communion (once per month), teaching or preaching. The
question I have is this; what if God wanted to do something
different? What if God wanted us to spend the whole meeting on our faces in repentance? Or what if God wanted a
whole meeting of worship, or a whole meeting of just
prayer? You see, my friend, what we do on a regular basis
is try to cram so many things into our meetings that we push
God right out the door! There's no room left for Christ.
This is what we're really doing: *we are playing church*!

We set up our system and then we do it our way and in our
time frame. Where is the Holy Spirit in all that? Sadly
enough, He is usually out the door.

Do we really want the Spirit to move in our meetings? I
believe we do. Wouldn't it be exciting to have people visit
the church and be totally blown away by the sence of God
in His people?

> "And thus the secrets of his heart are
> revealed; and so, falling down on his face, he
> will worship God and report that God is truly
> among you." I Cor. 14:25

In order to have Christ in charge of the meeting, we need to seek Him *before* the meeting to find out what He wants for that particular gathering of His church. We need to be flexible in order to be led by the Spirit spontaneously and not to pre-program the meetings. Don't assume anything. Don't slip back into comfortable patterns or programs just because you're not sure where to go next. Don't rush God. He's not in a hurry. Don't be afraid. If we put our trust in Him and allow Him to lead, He will surely do it; after all, He's the head.

Every Member Responsible

As we have already seen, Paul wrote his letters to the whole church, not to a leader or a group of elders. In Corinthians, chapters 11 – 14, Paul is trying to correct some wrong practices in regards to their meetings. Now . . . listen to this. He never once directs these corrective remarks to anyone other than the *whole* church! In other words, the *whole* church was responsible to make sure that the meetings were run in a decent and orderly fashion. This can lead us to only one conclusion; there was no one person who was responsible to lead these meetings! If there had been certainly Paul would have directed his corrections to that person who was supposed to be in charge. We never see Paul telling Gaius (in whose house the meetings were) to straighten out the situation or he would be replaced as the leader. We only see him directing everything he said to the whole church. In fact, Paul never indicates anywhere in his writings that there were to be any human leaders in any of the meetings. Christ led the meetings through His Spirit. All of the believers participated and all of them ministered. This is exciting!

There is one ingredient that I believe should be in all church meetings. This is one thing that you can always begin with and rely on that God will bless: worship. It is out of our worshipping God that all other ministry will spring forth. If we put Christ at the center of the meeting and come loving Him, and allow God to move as He will, we can be sure of having some wonderful meetings.

Purpose for Meetings

Even though worship is very important, we must realize that worship is not the reason why we gather together. Paul teaches that worship is offering up our whole lives to God (see Ro. 12:1, 2). We don't come together primarily to worship because our whole life is to be an act of worship. We should just continue that flow of worship when we come to meetings.

In addition, church, or the gathering together of believers, is not for the purpose of mission or evangelism. That is supposed to be happening outside of the meetings. Of course, if an unbeliever comes into the meeting, God can save him right where he is. However, this is a byproduct of the church sharing the word with one another as in I Cor. 14: 24, 25. Evangelism and social action should primarily take place in the everyday life of the believer.

So what *is* the main purpose for us to gather together as believers? *It is for the purpose of edification of the members through their God-given ministry to one another.*

As I shared before, we don't come to the meetings to receive, we come to give. We can only do this if we have something to give! That's why we must have a deep, living, vibrant experience of walking with Christ in our daily lives. If we don't, then we really have nothing to give. You see, the reason we come together is to share our experience of Christ with one another.

> "Let all things be done decently and in order." I Cor. 14:40

The meetings of the church are not to be free-for-alls. There is an order for every meeting and all things must be done decently. Every part or member is to be given freedom to minister as God leads. I Cor. 14:26 makes this very clear. Every member of the body is important and every believer should flow in his/her ministry on a regular basis in the meetings. As we gather together we should see Christ Himself being expressed as all of the individual members participate in worship and ministry. Why does only one person need to bring a teaching? Why can't several believers share things from the scriptures as the Holy Spirit leads them? By the way, there is no mention of a song leader or worship leader in the first century church. That's because *all* the saints lead out in songs and sang to God and one another during the meetings.

> ". . . speaking to one another in psalms and hymns and spiritual songs, singing and making melody with your heart to the Lord." Ephesians 5:19

Just like everything else in the meetings, the *whole* church led the songs. Why can't several people share music and testimonies, prayers, revelations, messages, etc.? Just think what interesting meetings we would have! Everyone would be involved and flowing in their gifts and ministries. This way people would not only receive but give ministry as well. Remember what Jesus said, "It is more blessed to give than to receive." In modern church meetings, the people just sit there and receive all the time. They are missing out on the "true" blessing of *giving* ministry instead of just receiving. God wants an *activated* priesthood! What good is it that we are priests if all we do is sit there and watch like an audience at a show? It's time for all leaders to train, encourage, and open the way for all the believers to participate in ministry during the meetings. The meetings of the church are where the people learn to move in their gifts so that they can flow over into use in their everyday lives.

You might be thinking, "This will never happen because the people will never get involved." How do you know? The believers will participate if they are encouraged and allowed to. Of course, this might be difficult in the beginning because Christians are so used to sitting back and letting someone else do all the work. But as they step out in faith, they will see what a blessing it is to be used of God and will want to do more. The church has been stuck in this rut for centuries so it's going to take some time to change old habits.

Endless Variety

In order for us to have meetings like I am describing here,

they need to be small enough for intimate fellowship and interaction among the members. Now in case you didn't know it, the early church met in homes. That's right. In fact there were no church buildings constructed until the fourth century. The typical first century living room could hold about 30-40 people. The larger homes like that of Gaius in Corinth (see Ro. 16:23) could hold about 50 people at the maximum. The house of Gaius was used when the whole church came together in Corinth. Apparently, smaller groups also got together at other times in that city. The point here is that the meetings were small to facilitate the ministry interaction among the members. This is vitally important. We have lost a great treasure by making our meetings large and centering our ministries around buildings.

Another important thing for us to understand is that these meetings should have an endless amount of variety. If Christ is allowed to lead the meeting, then all the gatherings will definitely not be the same. There will be no set pattern or ritual that is practiced in every meeting. Our Father has deposited an infinite amount of creativity and variety within His Son and all of that is to be expressed through the church.*

Individual brothers and sisters can share songs, teachings, scriptures, stories, poems, etc. Groups of believers can get together and present Christ through a dramatic or musical

----

* See the book "The Coat of Many Colors" by the author for a more detailed description of the variety within the body of Christ.

production. The whole meeting can be mobile and go to a particular sister's house to pray for her and sing to her. The whole church can meet someone arriving at the airport and greet them with song and prayer. There is literally no end to the different ways that we can meet. All the sisters can take the meeting and do something special for the brothers. Or the brothers could do something for the sisters. The church can have "special" meetings for the Lord's Supper where they rent out a hall and have a literal feast and invite their neighbors and people in need. The only limit is the imagination and creativity of our Lord!

Community life

Now we need to realize that the meetings are just a small part of church life. The same flow of worship, fellowship, love, giving, ministry, and caring is to continue between meetings as well. We are to share our very lives in common. In fact, we don't absolutely have to have meetings to be a church. This means that church life is a continual flow of God's Spirit among the members. This means that between the meetings, believers are getting together, having each other over for a meal and fellowship, praying together, ministering to one another, and sharing as the need arises. The church is a family and that means relationships. We're not a club! This is a loving, caring family that loves to be together, not only that, but we have lots of fun together! Communication needs to flow freely so that ministry can be extended to those in need at the time of the need, not a week later at a meeting when it may be too late. If all the believers are functioning as priests and ministers, then needs can be met quickly and easily instead of some pastor having to be at six places at one time. Why call in a doctor when the body can heal itself? The church is a life, not just a meeting.

Now I believe that if the meetings function the way that they are supposed to, then the believers will want to be together outside of the meetings as well. During the meetings, people will learn to care for their brothers and sisters and this will cultivate a love between them that will surely extend outside of the meetings. Of course, the type of meeting I'm referring to has to be small enough for there to be personal ministry and relationships develop. This usually cannot happen in large church gatherings. What I am discussing here is small home meetings of probably no more than twenty or thirty believers. It is in these informal meetings that personal, intimate, relationships and ministry can develop. The believers can learn to use their gifts and love one another at the same time. The gifts and the fruit of the Holy Spirit will develop simultaneously, as they are supposed to. The power, authority, and character of Christ will be expressed through His church. The fullness of Christ will be made visible!

Now come with me as we make an imaginary visit to one of these meetings.

The door of the house opens and you are greeted by a smiling brother who gives you a big hug. As you enter the living room you see about a dozen people, all talking and laughing and having an extremely good time. You quickly join in with the fun. Two sisters start singing a song to the Lord together. At first, the rest of the group doesn't notice because they are too busy chatting with one another. But then the two women are joined with a third, then a fourth sister, all singing along. The rest of the group now quiet down and one by one, start joining in the song to the Lord. One brother has a guitar and begins playing. Another sister has an Autoharp and begins strumming along. Now the whole room is full of voices expressing their praise and love to their Lord. Several saints have now stood up and are lifting their hands to the Lord. Several sisters sitting on a couch have their arms around one another and are swaying to the rhythm of the music as their smiling, singing faces are turned upward.

Between songs, words of praise pour forth out of their mouths like a gentle breeze. The saints begin to declare the glory and greatness of the Christ who lives within them. You begin to sense God's presence filling the room and can't help weeping as His love and power surround you. You feel like you could go on forever like this, praising and worshipping Him, ministering to God as a priest. Another saint leads a song and the peace of God fills your spirit as you focus all of your attention on Him. All of the stress and hectic activity of the day is now forgotten as you rest in the peace that surpasses all understanding. In this quiet time, someone speaks a gentle prophecy of comfort and encouragement to the whole group. One of the sisters walks over to another sister, lays her hand on her shoulder, and speaks a word of comfort and edification by explaining to her that Christ *is* her comfort.

One of the brothers opens his bible and begins reading a passage of scripture out loud. Another sister begins to sing a song. This is not a song that anyone has ever heard before. She is singing a new (prophetic) song to the Lord! She is declaring through song the victory that Christ won on the cross. All of a sudden, people start clapping and shouting their praises for His glorious victory. The whole place is exploding with joy and triumphant praise.

As things quiet down and people start sitting down, a sister begins to share her experience of the Lord that she had that week. One by one, brothers and sisters are sharing their encounters with the Lord from the last few days. Three sisters stand up and share a song that they wrote during the week. Then another brother leads a song that they all sing together. One sister shares that she senses God wanting the group to pray for one of the other sisters. The group gets up and gathers around this sister and begins to pray. One brother has a word of exhortation and wisdom for this sister. Another sister prays for an emotional healing to take place. The sister that is being ministered to is obviously being touched by the Lord in some deep areas of need. Some other prayers are spoken and then several saints hug this sister.

A married couple asks for prayer. The group huddles around them and then sings a song to them. The wife begins to weep. Several of the sisters begin praying for her while they hold her hands. Jesus Christ is on the lips of every saint. This is *not* man-centered ministry. This is Christ-centered ministry where all attention is brought to Christ, all glory is given to Christ, and all hearts are toward Christ. The couple receives true healing because it is Christ who is being ministered. People's personal problems are never discussed or analyzed because this is *not* a counseling session. This is Christ ministering to the needs of His body! The body is edifying itself in love.

Now a sister leads in a song and everyone joins in. A brother shares something that the Lord gave him in the scriptures for a few minutes. Then another brother leads in another song and the group begins to stand as they join arm in arm in several choruses of "Amazing Grace." The meeting is ended and everyone is back to chatting and laughing.

You think to yourself, wow! What a meeting! But actually, this is just a normal one!

CHAPTER THIRTEEN

KINGS AND PRIESTS FOREVER

It's very important that you and I understand who we are and where we are going in Christ. What is God's ultimate goal for the church?

Our Eternal Destiny

First we need to realize that God is primarily concerned with eternity. Of course, He cares about the here and now because that will determine, in a large part, what happens throughout eternity. Most Christians don't really comprehend the glorious position and ministry that the church will have in eternity. Most Christians can only think about going to heaven someday. But guess what? Heaven is only a temporary place! That's right, I said that heaven is only a temporary place for the church as well as the throne of God! Let's take a look at some scriptures.

> "Heaven and earth will pass away, but My words will by no means pass away."
> Matthew 24:35

"Then one of the seven angels who had the seven bowls filled with the seven last plagues came to me and talked with me, saying, "Come, I will show you the bride, the Lamb's wife." And He carried me away in the Spirit to a great and high mountain, and showed me the great city, the holy Jerusalem, descending out of heaven from God, having the glory of God." Rev. 21:9-11a

"But I saw no temple in it, for the Lord God Almighty and the Lamb are its temple. And the city had no need of the sun or of the moon to shine in it, for the glory of God illuminated it, and the Lamb is its light." Rev. 21:22, 23

"And He showed me a pure river of water of life, clear as crystal, proceeding from the throne of God and of the Lamb. In the middle of its street, and on either side of the river, was the tree of life, which bore twelve fruits each tree yielding its fruit every month. And the leaves of the tree were for the healing of the nations. And there shall be no more curse, but the throne of God and of the Lamb shall be in it, and His servants shall serve Him. They shall see His face, and His name shall be on their foreheads. And there shall be no night there; they need no lamp nor light of the sun, for the Lord God gives them light. And they shall reign forever and ever." Rev. 22:1-5

It is very obvious that the throne of God is in the city of the New Jerusalem and that this city comes down out of heaven to the earth. The church will then reign forever and ever with Christ with the New Jerusalem being the center from which this will take place. Exactly what we will be doing and how we will rule with Christ is not explained. We do know, however, that God's ultimate goal for the church is to rule and reign with Christ over His kingdom. The church is called the bride, the Lamb's wife. God's whole purpose in sending Christ to die on the cross was to give birth to this bride-to-be, an eternal companion for His Son. As foreshadowed in the Garden of Eden, God saw that it was not good for His Son, the second Adam, to be alone, so He called out an eternal companion for Him, the church. Not only will the church be an eternal companion for the Son, she will also be co-regent or co-ruler with Christ over His kingdom. This is totally mind-boggling!

The Training of the Bride

This means that everything that God has done in time past, is doing right now, and will continue to do until the Marriage Supper of the Lamb (Rev. 19:9) is for the purpose of calling forth, training, preparing, and maturing the Bride of Christ for her destiny as co-regent of the universe.

All of God's dealings with His people are for the purpose of "on-the-job training" in order to teach them how to overcome and apply the Supreme Law of the universe: eternal love. Only the overcomer can rule.

> "To him who overcomes, I will grant to sit
> with Me on My throne, as I also overcame
> and sat down with My Father on His throne."
> Rev. 3:21

This is why God allows two agents to affect our lives: the devil and suffering or tribulation.

Jesus completely and legally defeated satan and all his works on the cross of Calvary. satan became an "official" murderer when he killed a completely innocent man. He now has no rights or legal claim over those who are born from above and washed in the blood of the Lamb. So why does God still allow him to harass and run around causing trouble? The reason is that God is using satan for the purpose of on-the-job training in order to prepare His church to rule the universe with Him. Through the vehicle of prayer, God wants us to learn to implement His will on the earth. "Thy kingdom come, Thy will be done, on earth as it is in heaven." (Also see Matthew 18:18, 19) By persevering in prayer, pulling down strongholds, and binding and loosing, we become overcomers. This is experience we are going to need in order to rule with Christ.

Suffering

The second agent or tool, which God uses in our lives, is suffering or tribulation. The reason that God allows us to go through suffering is so that we will learn eternal love. This love is the supreme law of the kingdom (see I Cor. 13). Those who rule in God's kingdom can only do so according to this law of love.

This divine love must be worked into our character through the various trials and tribulations which we go through.

> "If we endure, we shall also reign with Him."
> II Timothy 2:12a

> "You therefore must endure hardship as a good soldier of Jesus Christ." II Timothy 2:3

> ". . . and if children, then heirs – heirs of God and joint heirs with Christ, if indeed we suffer with Him, that we may also be glorified together." Romans 8:17

> "For our light affliction, which is but for a moment, is working for us a far more exceeding and eternal weight of glory, while we do not look at the things which are seen, but the things which are not seen. For the things which are seen are temporary, but the things which are not seen are eternal."
> II Cor. 4:17, 18

> "And not only that, but we also glory in tribulations, knowing that tribulation produces perseverance; and perseverance, character; and character, hope. Now hope does not disappoint, because the love of God has been poured out in our hearts by the Holy Spirit who was given to us." Romans 5:3-5

The Law of Love

So you see that God uses suffering in our lives to develop love within us. Without this being built into our character, we would not be equipped to rule in His kingdom because love is the supreme law by which all rule and authority is to be implemented. Love is the fulfillment of the law (see Gal. 5:14). Of course, the tribulation, which God brings into our lives, will not serve its purpose unless we receive it and yield to His dealings. If all we do is complain and murmur and resist His dealings, then we will be wasting these sorrows that were meant for our good (Romans 8:28). We must learn to glory in our tribulations just as Paul did.

"Rejoice always, pray without ceasing, in everything give thanks; for this is the will of God in Christ Jesus for you."
I Thes. 5:16-18

CHAPTER FOURTEEN

SPIRITUAL WARFARE

In the last chapter we touched upon our eternal position and ministry with Christ. We will now take a look at the spiritual authority He has given His Bride for her eternal ministry. Remember, God didn't send Christ to die on the cross so that when we die we could go to heaven, float on a cloud, and play a harp all the time. God has a definite plan for eternity in which Christ and His church will rule the universe together. We don't know what all this means yet, but you can be sure of one thing; in order for Jesus Christ to allow His church to co-rule with Him, she is definitely going to have to be prepared and trained for such an awesome responsibility. As we already saw in Revelation 3:21, it is only the overcomer who will be allowed to sit on His throne. The time that we learn to overcome is right now. While we live on this earth for our seventy or eighty years, God is continually trying to teach us to overcome. This word overcome can also be translated conquer in Rev. 3:21. We cannot rule until we have first conquered! This principle is beautifully illustrated for us in the life of David. He had to overcome as a warrior before he became a king. He had to defeat the armies of the enemy territories around him so that his kingdom would be established. He did this by obedience to the Lord and in the power of His might. The Lord fought the battles; all David had to do was obey Him. This brings up a point that needs to be addressed.

Shift Needed in Our Paradigm

The popular concept of spiritual warfare that we have today in the church is definitely not the same as they had in the first century. The way we think about spiritual warfare today is basically taken from ideas and philosophies from the world system more than from the New Testament. We need a major paradigm shift in the way we think of spiritual warfare.

Our modern day thinking about spiritual warfare consists of a dichotomy that pits good against evil, light against darkness, and God against satan. While the basis of this idea is true, we usually go beyond this to believe that the forces of good and evil are equally balanced and that somehow the church is caught in the middle and the outcome will be determined by our perseverance, or commitment to prayer, or some other such nonsense. This concept nullifies and emasculates the power of the cross. Most of us have no idea of the degree of completeness that God accomplished in Christ on the cross.

> "[God] disarmed the principalities and powers ranged against us and made a bold display and public example of them, in triumphing over them in Him and in it [the cross]."
> Colossians 2:15 (Amplified)

God accomplished complete victory over all the power of the evil one through Christ on the cross. His victory was total and complete. All Christians know this but do we really believe it? If we believe it then our lives will follow suit.

Please do not misunderstand me. We do "wrestle" against an enemy. But that "wrestling" is not against flesh and blood, and therefore, the rules of our warfare are not according to the rules of this world system.

The victory has already been won by Christ. Now the church is to demonstrate and express that victory. We are not to run from the devil, but neither are we to engage him according to his terms or by his rules. Our warfare is spiritual, not carnal. We pull down strongholds by standing upon the established truth that on His cross He completely defeated satan and his hosts. The church is to demonstrate this fact by living in His rest and not giving in to fear and chasing demons under every rock! The church is engaged in warfare, but that warfare is not fought like cowboys and Indians or Star Wars. Let's take a look at Paul's letter to the Ephesians to gain more insight into this matter.

> "Finally, be strong in the Lord, and in the strength of His might. Put on the full armor of God, that you may be able to stand firm against the schemes of the devil."
> Ephesians 6:10, 11

There are several things that we need to notice here about this famous passage concerning what we normally call "spiritual warfare."

The Body Puts the Armor On

First, we need to realize that Paul is speaking to the church, which is His body. He is not speaking to individuals. Today, we take this passage, as well as the rest of the New Testament, and apply it to ourselves as individuals. But it was not written to individuals, it was written to the body. Therefore, we can make the following conclusions.

The body is to put on the full armor of God. This is not an individual matter. She, the church, is the only one who is equipped to handle these things. If you try to stand against the devil on your own, you are going to be defeated, or at least get yourself beaten up!

What Armor?

Not only that, but what is it exactly that we are to "put on"? When we read further into this passage and see what the armor consists of, we find the following: truth, righteousness, gospel, peace, faith, salvation, and Spirit. Is not Jesus Christ all of these things? These are not "things" that are separate from Him and that we need to have and apply on our own. Our individualistic minds love to divide and separate things. But this armor is simply a description of your Lord! He is truth. He is righteousness. He is peace, faith, salvation, etc. Paul is simply telling the church(es) to put on Christ!

> "But put on the Lord Jesus Christ, and make
> no provision for the flesh in regard to its lust."
> Romans 13:14

"... and put on the new self (man), which in
the likeness of God has been created in righteousness and holiness of the truth."
Ephesians 4:24

In order to stand against the devil, we (as the body of Christ)
are to put on the Lord Jesus Christ. After having done this,
then we are simply to stand in Him. Saints, He is our Armor.
He is our Defense. He is our Fortress. And we put Him on
as a corporate body, not as individuals. The ironic thing
about this is that she should be putting on Christ anyway! If
Christ is being taken as her All, then there is not much need
to even think about spiritual warfare.

The Snake in the Fire

One story in the life of Paul beautifully illustrates this point.
This story takes place in Acts 28, when on his way to Rome.
Paul was shipwrecked and ended up on the island of Malta
off the coast of Sicily. He gathered together some sticks for
the fire and a viper came out and fastened on his hand. He
simply shook it off into the fire and suffered no harm. Notice
that Paul didn't ask for prayer, or start rebuking the snake in
the name of Jesus! He just shook it off and ignored it.

That's how we need to treat the devil. Just shake him off and
ignore him. Having put on Christ, the church only needs to
stand in Him and the victory that He has already won on the
cross.

CHAPTER FIFTEEN

PRIESTLY CONSECRATION

"Now the Lord called to Moses, and spoke to him from the tabernacle of meeting, saying, 'Speak to the children of Israel and say to them: "When any one of you brings an offering to the Lord, you shall bring your offering of the livestock – of the herd and of the flock. If his offering is a burnt sacrifice of the herd, let him offer a male without blemish; he shall offer it of his own free will at the door of the tabernacle of meeting before the Lord. Then he shall put his hand on the head of the burnt offering, and it will be accepted on his behalf to make atonement for him. He shall kill the bull before the Lord; and the priests, Aaron's sons, shall bring the blood and sprinkle the blood all around on the altar that is by the door of the tabernacle of meeting. And he shall skin the burnt offering and cut it into pieces. The sons of Aaron the priest shall put fire on the altar, and lay the wood in order on the fire. Then the priests, Aaron's sons, shall lay the parts, the head, and the fat in order on the wood that is on the fire upon the altar; but he shall wash its entrails and its legs with water. And the priest shall burn all on the altar as a burnt sacrifice, an offering made by fire, sweet aroma to the Lord.'" Leviticus 1:1-9

"Then Moses took some of the anointing oil and some of the blood which was on the altar, and sprinkled it on Aaron, on his garments, on his sons, and on the garments of his sons with him; and he consecrated Aaron, his garments, his sons, and the garments of his sons with him." Leviticus 8:30

I beseech you therefore, brethren, by the mercies of God that you present your bodies a living sacrifice, holy, acceptable to God, which is your reasonable service."
Romans 12:1

In the Levitical priesthood, before the priests could begin their service, they had to be consecrated. Consecrate means to set apart or dedicate something or someone for a specific purpose. Before Aaron and his sons could begin their ministry, they needed to be dedicated to the Lord's service and be set apart for His purpose for them. Moses took the priests and anointed them with oil, sprinkled the blood of the sacrifice on them and their garments, and later we are told that they also had to wash in water for the next seven days. All of these activities have spiritual significance for us today in our New Covenant priesthood.

The Sprinkling of the Blood

Moses was told by God to take the blood from the animal sacrifice and sprinkle it on Aaron, his sons, and their garments. Later on in Leviticus, Moses tells us that the life is in the blood and the blood is identified with its life. (Lev. 17:11, 14) On the cross, the blood of Christ was poured out for us. His blood, His *life*, was poured out so that we could receive that life and live by that life. He said that He was the Bread of life (John 6:48) and that just as He lived by the life of His Father, so could we live by His (Christ's) life if we ate Him. (John 6:57)

The first thing that must happen with a group of believers before they can function as a priesthood is that the life of Christ must flow through the body. His blood, if you will, must flow through the veins of His body. Without His life, we are just another dead institution. Human life can never do this thing! Our priesthood is after the order of Melchizedek and this priesthood is based upon the power of an indestructible life (Heb. 7:16). There is only one kind of life that is indestructible and that is resurrected life. It is life that has conquered death! Every individual believer needs to learn to live by this life instead of his/her own human life. Then we will see the priesthood of Melchizedek live again.

The Washing in Water

Water also speaks of His life but brings with it some additional aspects that we need to see with our spirits.

Thirst

Water not only gives life, but it also quenches our thirst. As we know, our human bodies are made up of at least 90% water. So also is the body of Christ! His body is filled with His life, but in order for the priesthood to come forth in a local expression of the body, there must be a thirst in the brothers and sisters. If there is a genuine thirst for Him among the believers, then the Living Waters can flow into the body and fill her up, even to overflowing. The overflow of life will touch those who are outside the body that God is drawing to enter in.

Flowing

Water not only supplies drink to the thirsty, it also can flow like a river to supply the needed nourishment to dry and parched lands.

In the Garden of Eden we see the River of life. This river represents that which exists inside of the living God. Inside of God, there is a river (flowing) of life that is circulating among the Father, the Son, and the Spirit. The One who initiates and energizes this flow is the Holy Spirit. There is a continuous flow of divine life being given and received among the Persons of the Godhead. This flow of divine life is what we call fellowship (Koinonia), and that is to be the basis for the flow of life within the church.

> "What was from the beginning, what we have heard, what we have seen with our eyes, what we beheld and our hands handled,

concerning the Word of life – and the life was manifested, and we have seen and bear witness and proclaim to you the eternal life, which was with the Father and was manifested to us – what we have seen and heard we proclaim to you also, that you also may have fellowship with us; and indeed our fellowship is with the Father, and with His Son Jesus Christ." I John 1:1-3

The Anointing with Oil

Oil always symbolizes the Holy Spirit in the scriptures. The word 'Christ' means 'Anointed One.' The Holy Spirit was poured out upon, in, and through Jesus Christ. The Father's full anointing rests upon Him. When the Holy Spirit descended upon Him at His baptism, He was completely covered or immersed in the Spirit. This was a man who was led completely by the Spirit. This was a man who walked in the Spirit completely and perfectly. This was a man who exercised all the gifts of the Spirit. And this was a man who bore all the fruit of the Spirit. He not only did, and manifested all these things, He *is* all these things!

The Spirit descended on the day of Pentecost so that the church, which is His body, could be indwelt by this same Son of Man. He now entered His body by His Spirit so that the church could express who He is. She, the church, is to manifest the power of the Spirit by allowing Christ to live within and through her.

Now Christ must have the preeminence in all things. He must have the preeminence in the church. He is either Lord of all or not Lord at all! You see, dear saint, God has purchased us with the precious blood of Jesus. We no longer belong to ourselves. We are now God's own possession. We belong to Him. How could we ever live for ourselves? In fact, Paul said that he no longer lives but Christ lives in him. This is the "secret" of the Christian life. It's not our life at all! It's His life in us. All we need to do is give complete control to the Holy Spirit. He does the rest. If we seek to live by His life and walk in fellowship with Him, then the Holy Spirit will lead us and all we need to do is obey His promptings. This is what the Bible calls walking in the Spirit.

There are two important ways in which we learn to follow the leadings of the Holy Spirit, church life and personal fellowship with the Lord. As we have already seen, church life is very important in the life of the believer. The church is to be the container for the life of God. This is lived out individually and corporately. Our corporate life together is very vital because it is there that the believers will be encouraged and strengthened to live out the individual walk with God. God never intended for us to be spiritual lone rangers! The church is God's family and we are to develop intimate relationships with other brothers and sisters and help one another to learn to overcome. This is how we learn to serve. This is how we learn to love.

CHAPTER SIXTEEN

THE SECRET PLACE

"He who dwells in the secret place of the Most High shall abide under the shadow of the Almighty." Psalm 91:1

"You shall hide them in the secret place of Your presence, from the plots of man; You shall keep them secretly in a pavilion from the strife of tongues." Psalm 31:20

Scripture speaks of this secret place many times in various descriptions. What is this mysterious, secret place and where can we find it? Adam, Noah, Abraham, Moses, Elijah, Dvid, Dniel, John the Baptist, Jesus, Peter, and Paul all went there. It was the "secret" weapon of their success. If it hadn't been for this place, none of them would have gone anywhere! They were completely hidden from the eyes of the world when they were in this place. No one could touch them when they were in this place. This place was so revolutionary in their lives that each time they went there, they would be changed! In fact they could not go there without being changed.

What could this place be? Is it a building? Is it a town or country? Is it the tabernacle or temple? Is it a mountain retreat?

The secret place is the presence of God!

It is only as we learn to live and walk in His presence that we will be changed into His likeness. Notice that I said *we* will be changed into His likeness or image. The image of God is a corporate matter, not just for individual believers.

> "But whenever Moses went in before the Lord to speak with Him, he would take the veil off until he came out; and he would come out and speak to the children of Israel whatever he had been commanded. And whenever the children of Israel saw the face of Moses, that the skin of Moses' face shone, then Moses would put the veil on his face again, until he went in to speak with Him." Ex. 34:34, 35

> "But *we all*, with unveiled face, beholding as in a mirror the glory of the Lord, are being transformed into the same image from glory to glory, just as by the Spirit of the Lord." I Cor. 3:18

We all! The spiritual walk is a *"we all"* thing. Please keep in mind that this is for the church, the body of Christ.

This story in Exodus is a beautiful picture of how God

changes us into His image when we are in His presence. The face of Moses actually shone with a brightness after he had spent time communing with the Lord. The Bible says that God is light. Our brothers and sisters, this is the one sure-fire way for us to be changed into His likeness. All other things or activities will flow out of this secret place. You can receive teaching for years without ever being changed. You can read your Bible for years without ever being changed. You can even preach and minister to others for years without ever being changed. The only place that will change you is God's presence. You will be changed in that place!

Now dear saints, you must realize that all of the things that I have shared in the previous chapters can be used to try and have church life. But the outward things cannot bring life. When I say outward things, I am speaking of the usual means that we try and use to propel our spiritual walk. Such things as bible study, prayer, speaking in tongues, spiritual gifts, ministries, witnessing, giving, scripture memorization, meditating on the Word, going to church, etc. are not to be the means or engine that energizes our spiritual lives. These things are the *result* of life, not the source! You must understand this very important point: *it all must begin in Christ! He* is our life. You must start there. If you don't have an intimate, personal, habitual fellowship with God in your spirit, then there will be nothing that can flow out to others. Christ is the center and source of all we do. Christ is *supreme*. Christ is our all in all. It all begins with an inward fellowship of His Spirit with our spirit. From this life comes everything that flows outwardly.

Now, because we are all priests we can enter into intimate fellowship with God just like the New Testament saints. We can speak face to face with Him as we enter into the Holy of holies right before His throne.

> "Therefore, brethren, having boldness to enter the Holiest by the blood of Jesus, by a new and living way which He consecrated for us, through the veil, that is, His flesh, and having a High Priest over the house of God, let us draw near with a true heart in full assurance of faith, having our hearts sprinkled from an evil conscience and our bodies washed with pure water." Hebrews 10:19-22

Where is the Secret Place?

It's important that we discover the location of the "secret place" as well as how to get there. It's true that Jesus told us that He would never leave us and would always be with us. But there is a place that He inhabits that is even closer and more specific than that.

> "Christ in you, the hope of glory . . ." Col. 1:27b

Christ, actually, literally lives inside of you! The Father placed His Son inside of your spirit when you first believed. He gave you a spirit for this very purpose. It's the place where you and He can fellowship. His Spirit has joined together with your spirit and now they are one. (I Cor. 6:17)

Jesus said that He was going to prepare a place for us

(John 14:23). This place is in His Father's house. Do you really think that He is "up" there in heaven right now building you your own personal, private mansion? The Father's house is the church! He has prepared a place for you inside of her and that place is called 'spirit'. That's where the "secret place" is located. It is found within your spirit and the spirits of your brothers and sisters. That is where you go to fellowship with Him.

You see, this inward walk with Christ was the secret of the New Testament saints. They did not allow the outward circumstances to control or affect them in any way. Just look at the life of Paul. He didn't care if he was poor, or persecuted, or had to suffer loss. These were all outward things that had no affect upon his inward life at all. Just listen to him describe some of the things he went through:

> "Three times I was beaten with rods; once I was stoned; three times I was shipwrecked; a night and a day I have been in the deep; in journeys often; in perils of waters, in perils of robbers, in perils of my own countrymen; in perils of the Gentiles; in perils in the city; in perils in the wilderness; in perils in the sea; in perils among false brethren; in weariness and toil; in sleeplessness often; in hunger and thirst; in fastings often; in cold and nakedness – besides the other things, what comes upon me daily; my deep concern for all the churches." II Cor. 11:25-28

Paul was unstoppable! The reason for this was that he did

not allow any outward thing to have control over him. He was a man controlled by the Holy Spirit. We desperately need men and women like this today. Jesus said that from our innermost being shall flow rivers of living water. This will be the testimony of our daily walk as we learn to fellowship with Him by living in His Spirit. He is that river of living water. This is a matter of developing a habit. The habit of abiding in Christ. The habit of practicing His presence everyday in our lives. The habit of allowing His life to be lived through us.

> "And Enoch walked [n habitual fellowship] with God; and he was not, for God took him [ome with Him] Genesis 5:24 (Amp.)

> "Noah was a just and righteous man, blameless in his [vil]generation; Noah walked in habitual fellowship with God."
> Genesis 6:9 (Amp.)

CONCLUSION

As you can see, we have a great inheritance as a priesthood in Christ. God has called us *all* to love Him *and* serve Him as priests. Every member in the body is to function freely under the headship of Jesus Christ. That can only happen as we make Christ central and preeminent in the church. As I have stated before, it must be His life that gives birth to and sustains our lives together. This will not and cannot happen in our present day structures and mindsets. We not only need a paradigm shift, we also need a new wineskin. But what good is a new wineskin if we have not yet discovered where the wine is located and how to drink?

Radical Revolution Needed

What is needed today is much more than a reformation or a revival. As always, reformations are only partial restorations. Revivals are only temporary. What is needed in our generation is much more severe and radical than that. We need a radical revolution!

The word 'revolution' means a total and radical change in something that now exists. It implies a complete turnover or replacing of one form of government for another. That's what is needed today. We need a complete turnover of one government for another completely new one. The government of man, institutions, and the world system in the church must be torn down and the government of God must take its place. Of course, I am referring to the kingdom of God here. In His kingdom, He rules! Jesus Christ is the King and sovereign Head over His people. No man, nor system of man, should ever replace His complete Lordship and Headship in the church. He must be her Center, life, and Head in all things.

A reformation only attempts at changing or 'reforming' the current system. That will never work. The organized church system that we see today is way too far-gone and corrupt for reformation to be a viable solution. Many have tried and failed at changing the institutional church system. And should we even try? God is meeting those people where they are at. Who are we to try and disrupt that?

We can see that the present wineskins are not fit to hold the new wine. Patching up the old wineskin will never work. We need a completely new wineskin. We must begin afresh with a two-fold revelation as our guide.

The Eternal Purpose of God

As I stated in the beginning of this book, the expression of the church must always fit God's eternal purpose. She will always express Christ and if you do not see Christ being expressed in His fullness, then you do not have the true church, you have something less. If the church is not free to express her Lord as body, bride, temple, family and community, then you have something that does not fit into God's purpose. There is one particular aspect of this expression that I have focused on in this book and that is the priesthood of all believers. This means the freedom of all believers to express Christ by becoming functioning members as the body of Christ. However, this is just one aspect of the full expression of Christ in this realm. The Father wants to fill all things with Christ and He has chosen the church as the vehicle of this purpose. Anything less than this does not fit into His purpose.

The New Testament Story

The second aspect of our guiding revelation is, of course, the New Testament itself. But I am not referring to the chopped up way that we normally view our New Testament. The installation of chapters and verses has done us a disservice in at least two ways. One, it has "chopped up" the "story" of the first century and has almost made it impossible to discern what really went on there. Two, it has opened the door for every preacher and his brother to pull out a verse here and a verse there and come up with some pretty horrendous teachings that have clouded our vision of the story to an even greater degree.

When I say "story" I am speaking of the panoramic, holistic view of the first century church. We need to get the "big picture" to see what really happened then. Then we need the ability to place each incident in its proper context in consideration of the complete story.

We also need to have the historical, cultural, and sociological context for this story. The events in the first century church did not happen in a vacuum. It's important that we know where, why, and how things happened, all in relationship to the story as a whole. If we do this, we will never be able to fit our modern day church practices into this story.

A Missing Part – The Church Planter

One of the important "missing links" that we see all over the New Testament story and yet do not normally see today is the church planter (apostle, worker, sent-one). And yet they are the ones who raised up the churches in century one! Every church in the New Testament was either planted directly by an itinerant worker or was helped by one soon after its birth.

It is not in the scope of this book to cover in detail the calling and sending and work of church planters. However, we cannot talk about revolution in our day without them. They are the ones who will be leading this revolution because they are the ones who will be planting first century-styled churches!

I am not referring here to some huge church planning movement that will cover the earth with thousands of workers and tens of thousands of churches. Man always looks for quantity. God always looks and works for quality. Paul only planted around fifteen churches. He considered his work to be done after that. How could this be? Why didn't he want to duplicate his efforts and raise up thousands? It's because of the quality. Here again, we must remember God's eternal purpose.

What was important to Paul was the *measure of Christ* in each local assembly, not the quantity of assemblies. He knew that if Christ was being fully expressed through those churches, growth and expansion would just be the natural, organic byproduct. But this doesn't happen overnight. For Christ to be expressed through His body takes time. We are always concerned with numbers and speed. God does not have these concerns.

The Priesthood Resurrected

So, in order for us to see the priesthood of all believers restored to this earth we must have a revolution of the monumental kind. We must see a return to the eternal purpose of God as our driving force and vision and we must view the story of the first century church as one complete whole. May the Lord open our eyes to see these things that we may rise above our present day situations into His horizon of the full expression of His beloved Son.

Coming this Fall:

A New Book by Milt Rodriguez

"The Temple Within"

For more materials like this one, you can visit our

website at:

www.therebuilders.org

Published by The Rebuilders

2801 NW 23rd Blvd. #106
Gainesville, FL 32605
970-210-9795